PRODUCT MANAGEMENT IN SUPPLY CHAIN

Driving Efficiency, Innovation, and Quality

Olisaemeka Adigwe

Copyright © 2024 Olisaemeka Adigwe
Product Management in Supply Chain

All rights reserved. No part of this publication may be reproduced, transmitted, or stored in a retrieval system in any form or by any means, without permission in writing from the copyright holder.

Published in Nigeria in 2024 by Emphaloz Publishing House under its Emphaloz imprint

www.emphaloz.com

A catalogue record of this book will be available from the National Library of Nigeria.

technology, especially when the systems are large, old, or overstretched.

What makes the energy sector unique is that it doesn't move fast just for the sake of innovation. It moves fast because it has to. Energy is tied to economics, policy, infrastructure, and people's lives. That means product decisions carry more weight. That's why this book isn't about ideal models or perfect-case scenarios, it's about adapting principles to messy realities. And that's what makes strong product leaders so essential right now: they know how to hold the big picture in mind while navigating day-to-day volatility.

I won't pretend this book is exhaustive. It doesn't claim to cover every facet of the field. What it offers is a set of tools and perspectives grounded in years of practical work. You'll find frameworks, strategies, and examples that you can apply, challenge, or build upon. Some of these lessons came from successful projects. Others came from difficult moments; unexpected shutdowns, equipment failures, regulatory audits, and leadership gaps that forced me and my teams to rethink how we worked.

I've also included case-driven insights throughout, drawn from oil & gas operations, manufacturing plants, AI integration initiatives, and compliance transformations. These aren't generalized, they're meant to reflect the nuances that many in our field encounter but rarely have the time to document.

If you're a product manager trying to introduce new systems into legacy environments, this book will help you speak the language of operations. If you're an engineer transitioning into a broader product role, it will show you how to zoom out without losing your technical edge. If you're a supply chain professional navigating digital change, the chapters on AI, quality systems, and lifecycle design will offer practical grounding.

Above all, I hope this book reaffirms one simple truth: product management in supply chain is not about controlling everything, it's about connecting the right things. It's about aligning decisions with outcomes. It's about building systems that don't just function, but adapt, endure, and grow under pressure. This is the work I've committed myself to. And if you're reading this, chances are you're doing the same.

Foreword

In energy and manufacturing, product management isn't a clean, linear process. It's layered. You're coordinating between engineering specs, fluctuating inventories, real-time logistics, evolving safety standards, and, increasingly, digital systems that don't always speak to each other. I've led teams through all of it, from local refinery upgrades to multinational pipeline projects—and I can tell you this: the gap between design and delivery is where most operations stumble.

That's why this book is important.

Olisaemeka Adigwe has put together something rare here, an account of product management that doesn't treat the supply chain as an afterthought. Most management books focus on the ideal, the clean model, the universal solution. But in energy, no two environments are the same. Equipment ages differently. Regulation moves faster than infrastructure. Teams stretch themselves across operational silos. And leaders have to make decisions without perfect visibility.

This book starts in that reality and stays there.

Reading through the early chapters, it was clear that this wasn't just written by someone with product knowledge. It was written by someone who's been responsible for what happens when systems fail. Someone who's built maintenance schedules with AI and still walked the floor to talk to engineers about why things aren't moving. Someone who understands what it means to implement a new quality control process while also managing pressure from finance, logistics, and compliance, all at once.

That kind of range is hard to teach. But it can be documented. And Olisaemeka does just that.

He outlines where lifecycle management breaks down in manufacturing and how to rebuild it. He explores AI not as a buzzword, but as a decision tool that has to be integrated with intent. He walks through quality control and compliance from the perspective of someone who has had to justify both the standards and the budget in the same meeting. And in every chapter, he shows how leadership is less about controlling variables and more about aligning people, systems, and decisions under pressure.

In my own career, I've seen countless digital transformation efforts stall because they weren't grounded in operational context. Teams introduced new systems without considering what was already in place. Product managers pushed for automation without realizing the risk implications. Engineers were left translating between corporate strategy and field expectations. This book offers a better path; one that starts with understanding the environment before applying solutions.

What I also appreciate is how this book respects constraints. It doesn't assume you have unlimited resources or a blank slate. It assumes you're mid-process, mid-pressure, mid-deadline, and still expected to deliver.

If you're managing production across multiple locations, trying to keep your supply chain stable while integrating new systems, or navigating the tension between compliance and speed, this book will feel like a conversation you've had many times. And if you're leading product decisions in an environment where delay or defect has real consequences, it will sharpen how you think, not just about what to build, but how to sustain it.

This isn't a glossy guide to innovation. It's a grounded manual for those who make the real thing work.

Adeniyi Adesope

Reviews

Ayodele Omotayo
Senior Operations Engineer, Chevron Nigeria Ltd.

"This book isn't written from theory, it's built from field experience. Every chapter reflects problems I've faced and decisions I've had to make. Whether you're managing upstream logistics or downstream operations, Olisaemeka captures the complexity of supply chain product management in ways that are both technical and readable."

Adaora Nwankwo
Head, Digital Transformation – West Africa, Schneider Electric

"We often talk about digitizing supply chains in abstract terms. This book breaks it down. The chapters on AI integration and lifecycle efficiency go straight to the point, offering clarity for anyone leading transformation across physical and digital infrastructure."

Tunde Bako
Procurement & Supply Chain Manager, Oando Energy Resources

"I've worked in energy procurement for over a decade, and this is the first time I've seen product management principles applied so directly to our space. It bridges the gap between field operations and product strategy, something our sector has needed for a long time."

Zainab Lawal
Product Manager, Manufacturing Technology, Dangote Industries

"Most product management literature ignores the constraints of heavy industry. This one doesn't. It respects the complexity of scale, regulatory pressure, and legacy systems—while still offering real solutions."

Chijioke Umeh
HSE & Compliance Advisor, Nigerian National Petroleum Corporation (NNPC)

"The chapters on quality control, risk management, and compliance are worth the entire book. Olisaemeka doesn't just cover what's required, he shows how to make these systems functional without slowing down delivery."

Table of Contents

Preface III

Foreword VII

Reviews X

Table of Contents XII

Introduction XIII

CHAPTER 1: Foundations of Product Management in Energy Supply Chains 1

CHAPTER 2: Product Lifecycle Management in Manufacturing Operations 12

CHAPTER 3: Designing for Efficiency: Strategic Alignment in Supply Chains 32

CHAPTER 4: AI-Powered Optimization in Energy Product Management 45

CHAPTER 5: Intelligent Quality Control and Assurance Models 61

CHAPTER 6: Risk Management and Safety in Product Strategy 78

CHAPTER 7: Strategic Procurement and Supplier Management in
Product Delivery 89

CHAPTER 8: Sustainability and Circular Design in Supply Chain
Product Strategy 104

CHAPTER 9: Digital Transformation & Intelligent Systems in Product Lifecycle 118

CHAPTER 10: Building High-Performance Teams for Complex
Product Environments 130

About the Author 141

References 143

Introduction

Product management doesn't always begin with design sprints, prototypes, or sleek roadmaps. Sometimes, it begins in the middle of a broken process, with delays in delivery, a storage system no longer fit for scale, or a compliance audit that forces everyone to rethink how things are done. In the energy sector, that's often how it starts. Not as a proactive choice, but as a response to something that can no longer be ignored.

Over the past decade, I've had the opportunity to work across engineering, operations, and product strategy in the energy space, specifically in environments where product management is rarely visible, but absolutely essential. Refineries, storage terminals, manufacturing plants, transport hubs, places where product failures aren't just numbers in a dashboard, but disruptions with real consequences: cost overruns, safety risks, regulatory penalties, or stalled operations. That's the context that shaped this book.

We're used to seeing product management through the lens of digital companies; iterative, user-facing, fluid. But in industries like oil and gas, power, or manufacturing, product management looks and feels very different. It's tied to fixed assets, physical supply chains, legacy systems, regulatory frameworks, and high-stakes coordination. You don't get the luxury of shipping fast and fixing later. You have to get it right, and you have to do it while navigating around constraints most modern product literature doesn't even acknowledge.

That's the reality this book is built for.

Product managers in this space are expected to think long-term while responding to immediate problems. They manage trade-offs between safety and efficiency, speed and compliance, innovation and risk. They're responsible for keeping products viable not just through launch, but through maintenance, scale, and evolving customer demands, sometimes across decades.

In many ways, product management in energy is less about managing "products" and more about managing consequences.

This is especially true as supply chains grow more complex and fragile. Global interdependencies, price fluctuations, transportation bottlenecks, workforce shortages, digital infrastructure gaps, these are not just macroeconomic talking points. These are the things that directly impact how product decisions play out. And yet, many teams are still trying to navigate these challenges using outdated methods, siloed systems, or reactive thinking.

What this book offers is a way forward.

Each chapter is designed to offer insight into a specific domain of product management as it applies to energy-focused supply chains. But more importantly, each section is grounded in lived experience. You won't find theoretical diagrams with clean, uninterrupted flows. You'll find examples where things failed.

Where strategies were adjusted on the fly. Where teams had to work with incomplete data or systems that didn't talk to each other. And where the only way forward was to blend structure with adaptation.

We start with the foundations, understanding what product management looks like in heavy industry, and how it has to evolve to meet the needs of complex, multi-layered operations. We'll move into product lifecycle development, with a focus on planning for scale, integrating manufacturing workflows, and aligning product roadmaps with resource constraints. The goal is to take a broad function and break it down into actionable, environment-specific work.

As the book progresses, we'll dive into AI and data-driven optimization. Not from a high-level trend perspective, but from the lens of implementation: where AI has actually improved decision-making, how predictive analytics have helped reduce failure rates, and what it takes to integrate these systems into operations that still run partially on analog processes. These aren't case studies from Silicon Valley; they're drawn from oil and gas, where one misread sensor or unaddressed maintenance issue can shut down an entire site.

We'll also cover quality control, not as a checklist, but as a product strategy. The chapter explores how real-time monitoring, automation, and standardization can reduce cost, increase output reliability, and ensure compliance in tightly regulated environments. Quality isn't a department, it's a function that intersects with everything, from design to logistics to customer delivery.

Another important area is safety and risk management. In energy, this cannot be overstated. Products must be designed with compliance built in. Supply chains must be built around risk tolerance, not just speed. And teams must be trained not only on what to do, but on how to make judgment calls when conditions shift.

From there, we move into digitization. The conversations around smart factories, IoT, digital twins, and real-time data platforms are becoming louder; but implementation often lags. We'll explore what actually works, where the challenges lie, and how to make sure technology adoption leads to meaningful improvement, not more complexity.

Throughout the book, leadership and culture remain a recurring theme. Even the best product strategy will collapse under poor execution. And in large, industrial teams, often cross-generational, cross-functional, and cross-regional, the soft factors matter just as much as the hard ones. How teams align, how information is shared, and how decisions are made all contribute to whether a product survives, improves, or stalls.

The final chapter looks ahead, into the future of product management in the energy space. With sustainability becoming a core requirement, automation reshaping jobs, and resilience becoming a defining business priority, the role of the product manager must evolve. This book is part of that evolution.

But let's be clear, this isn't a quick-read leadership guide. It's not padded with motivational lines or overused frameworks. It's a working manual. It's for people who lead without perfect conditions. Who don't get to "pause and strategize" because the system needs to keep moving. It's for engineers who have found themselves managing product scope. For operations leaders trying to bring new systems online without slowing delivery. For product teams managing physical goods that take months to build, test, and deploy.

The energy sector is too complex for one-size-fits-all advice. What works in one facility might collapse in another. But there are patterns that repeat. Decisions that show up again and again. And lessons that, when applied correctly, can save time, money, and in some cases, lives.

If this book helps you make better decisions, more confidently, more clearly, and with fewer unknowns, then it has done its job.

CHAPTER 1

Foundations of Product Management in Energy Supply Chains

Product management in the energy sector rarely begins with a clean slate. It often starts with constraints, equipment that's already in place, systems that have been running for decades, processes with political and financial histories behind them, and expectations that do not always align with capacity. Unlike tech startups where a product manager can sketch a roadmap from scratch, product management in manufacturing and energy begins in motion. The plant is already running. The equipment is already in use. The logistics partners are already selected. And yet, something still needs to change, efficiency needs to improve, safety must be reinforced, output must scale, or a process must adapt to a new market condition. In this kind of environment, the role of a product manager is not to create from nothing, but to understand deeply, disrupt wisely, and build within systems that don't stop.

When we speak of "products" in the energy space, we are not talking about software apps or digital services. The product may be a processing unit, a mechanical component, a fuel container, a sensor network, or a bundled service involving transport, monitoring, and compliance. It may even be an internal operational process built to meet a regulatory standard. The product is often physical, often embedded, and always part of something larger. It cannot be considered in isolation. It must be managed within the context of asset constraints, safety protocols, supplier capabilities, and human factors. And it must meet its targets not just on paper, but in conditions that may include temperature extremes, erratic infrastructure, and real-time operational stress.

The product manager in this context does not operate as a feature manager or backlog owner. Their responsibility is systemic. They sit at the crossroads between engineering, operations, procurement, logistics, compliance, and customer delivery. They coordinate between teams that often do not share vocabulary, timelines, or tools. The engineer is thinking about flow rates and material durability. The procurement team is concerned with vendor risk and pricing. The compliance team is interpreting new regulations and asking how it affects production. The customer may be worried about availability or performance guarantees. The product manager must be fluent enough in each space to translate and align, not just for discussion, but for action.

What makes this work especially difficult is that product management in the energy sector must prioritize stability alongside innovation. Unlike industries where speed is the priority, energy and manufacturing prioritize reliability. You cannot fail fast if a failure means an environmental hazard, a multi-million dollar loss, or human injury. This doesn't mean innovation is impossible, but it must be handled differently. Change must be scoped, staged, and validated at every layer. Introducing a new component may require changes to maintenance schedules, training manuals, warehouse stocking practices, and regulatory documentation. A simple design tweak can trigger a cascading set of impacts across departments and systems.

At the same time, the product manager cannot afford to be reactive. Decisions must be made with foresight. Product lifecycles in this space are long, and misalignment during development can create persistent bottlenecks or safety issues downstream. This is why product managers must understand not just the product itself, but the infrastructure that delivers it, the systems that monitor it, and the people who maintain it. A product that is difficult to repair, requires specialized handling, or introduces unnecessary complexity into logistics is a weak product, no matter how well it performs in a test environment.

Supply chain integration is another foundational aspect of the role that cannot be overstated. In manufacturing and energy, the product does not exist outside of the supply chain, it lives within it. Raw materials availability can shift timelines. Component delays can stall installations. Port congestion can affect downstream revenue. A product that is not designed with the supply chain in mind will almost always create inefficiencies. This means the product manager must understand sourcing, vendor reliability, delivery timelines, and inventory control, not as background information, but as core inputs to product decisions. A change in the supply plan may require a reconfiguration of the product. A supplier quality issue may require an adjustment in the production process. Product development in this context is always iterative and dependent on supply realities.

Most conventional product management frameworks struggle under this kind of pressure. Agile methodologies built for rapid digital iterations do not map neatly onto physical products with long manufacturing lead times and rigid safety protocols. Iteration still happens, but it looks different. Feedback loops may take weeks or months. Testing requires real equipment, not virtual sandboxes. Field deployment might depend on maintenance windows that are scheduled months in advance. The product manager must work within these realities, finding creative ways to drive improvement without creating disruption.

Because of these challenges, successful product managers in energy supply chains often carry hybrid experience. Many started in engineering, project management, or operations. They understand what it means to work under resource constraints, to manage compliance documentation, or to sit in on risk assessment sessions. This background allows them to lead not with theoretical frameworks, but with practical judgment. They know when to push and when to wait. They understand how a decision in procurement might affect site logistics, or how a design flaw could create overtime costs for field teams. They think across silos. They lead through systems.

The foundation of product management in the energy sector, then, is not process, it is context. Understanding context allows the product manager to prioritize correctly, scope realistically, and execute reliably. It allows them to maintain credibility with technical teams while coordinating with executive stakeholders. It helps them deliver change in environments where failure is expensive and patience is short.

The clarity required in this role goes beyond internal documentation or meeting summaries. It means being able to clearly articulate what a product is meant to achieve, what it will require to succeed, and what trade-offs are involved in every version, revision, and release. In many traditional settings, this clarity can be theoretical, but in energy and manufacturing operations, it has to be practical. A product that adds operational strain is not a win, no matter how technically impressive it may be. Clarity, in this space, means designing with consequences in mind, consequences on site uptime, personnel workload, safety profiles, and the financial leeway of the organization.

The role also involves timing. Not everything that can be built should be built now. In fast-moving product spaces, timing often means beating competitors to market. In energy supply chains, timing is about alignment; ensuring that product changes or releases coincide with scheduled shutdowns, budget cycles, regulatory inspections, or new policy rollouts. For instance, a product that introduces new asset-tracking capabilities may not be adopted until the next planned equipment overhaul or digital system upgrade. That kind of delay isn't resistance, it's a necessary form of operational pacing. The product manager must read the rhythm of the organization and work with it, not against it.

Then there's the challenge of information flow. In many industrial settings, especially those involving legacy infrastructure, information isn't centralized. It's stored across spreadsheets, handwritten logs, disconnected systems, and informal knowledge embedded in long-serving personnel. In such environments, a product manager cannot assume they'll have a clean dataset or a comprehensive system of record. They have to dig. They have to observe what's not documented, listen to what isn't said in meetings, and ask questions others stopped asking years ago. This isn't just about gathering requirements, it's about uncovering operational truth.

Building credibility is part of that process. In environments where operational teams are constantly under pressure, the product manager doesn't automatically earn trust. They have to prove that their decisions will make the work easier, not harder. That their priorities aren't abstract but tied to real consequences. This means showing up where the work is happening, on the shop floor, in control rooms, during planning sessions. It means understanding what the night shift is doing differently from the day shift, and why. It means recognizing that a delayed shipment or a failed part isn't just a line on a report, it's overtime hours, backup plans, and lost momentum.

That depth of awareness is what separates surface-level coordination from actual product leadership. Without it, decisions are made in isolation, creating disjointed outcomes. A sensor is installed, but the maintenance team doesn't have access to its data. A new quality process is introduced, but it duplicates an inspection already happening at another checkpoint. A procurement switch is made, but the replacement part requires tools the site doesn't have. These are not hypothetical problems. They happen all the time when product management is practiced in name but not in substance.

To manage products in a supply chain-driven, energy-based context is to understand that the work doesn't stop at the interface. It extends into logistics, training, procurement, documentation, and continuous improvement. Product managers in this space are not only responsible for delivering a functional solution, but they are also responsible for ensuring that solution integrates into a larger system without creating friction. That's the real product: not the object, but the process and outcome it supports over time.

This kind of thinking leads to stronger decision-making over the long haul. It helps product managers prioritize not based on loudest voices, but based on system value. It prevents rushed launches that trigger downstream problems. It guards against shiny solutions that look good in presentations but collapse under the weight of operational complexity. And most importantly, it helps the organization build better habits; habits of testing assumptions, validating processes, coordinating across functions, and treating product development as a continuous, cross-cutting discipline.

The foundation of all this work is trust. Not just interpersonal trust, but operational trust. Trust that a new process won't make the job harder. Trust that system improvements won't compromise safety or overwhelm the team. Trust that when things go wrong, as they sometimes will, the product manager isn't simply managing optics but engaging directly with the people solving the problem. That trust is slow to build, easy to lose, and essential to success in this space.

1.1 Navigating Politics in Product Management

Every operational system is shaped by history. In supply chain-heavy environments, especially in state-linked or multi-partner energy ecosystems, product decisions are rarely just technical. They are political. That doesn't mean they're inherently dishonest or manipulative, but it does mean they're influenced by interests, priorities, and alliances that don't always align. A vendor may be tied to a long-standing relationship. A process might exist because it protected the organization in the past. A tool may be in place not because it works, but because removing it would offend the wrong stakeholder.

Product managers must learn how to read these dynamics without becoming consumed by them. It is not enough to propose a better system. You must understand who built the current one, why they still support it, and what it would mean, for them, politically and practically, if it were dismantled or changed. That level of awareness allows the product manager to build alignment instead of resistance. Sometimes this means bringing stakeholders into the design process early. Sometimes it means giving credit where it's due, even when the old system no longer serves. Sometimes it means choosing smaller changes that set the stage for bigger ones later. None of this is about appeasement. It's about sequencing change so that it lands and sticks.

This becomes even more important in organizations where hierarchy is strong and decision-making is layered. A product recommendation might have to pass through several levels of review, each with its own concerns. Operational heads might focus on cost, compliance teams on documentation, finance teams on return. The product manager becomes the thread, pulling together these perspectives and translating them into an approach that moves things forward without sparking institutional backlash. This requires a different kind of fluency, one rooted in awareness, timing, and the ability to ask not just what the system needs, but who the system is protecting.

1.2 Centralized Vision, Decentralized Ownership

Another common tension in energy-based product environments is the pull between centralization and autonomy. On one hand, product management requires clear ownership. There must be someone with a full view of scope, systems, and impact. On the other hand, supply chains are distributed. Operations are regional. Teams work under different conditions, with different suppliers, different constraints, and sometimes different cultures entirely. What works in one facility may not be translated to another. A centralized product strategy risks becoming too abstract. A fully localized one risks becoming fractured and inconsistent.

The product manager has to hold both realities at once. They must develop a product vision and delivery model that provides structure but allows room for interpretation. This might mean defining clear standards and outcomes but giving regional teams autonomy in how they achieve them. It might mean introducing a tool that integrates with existing workflows rather than replacing them outright. It might mean running pilots across multiple regions and collecting feedback before declaring a system-wide change.

Balancing these forces, control and flexibility, structure and feedback, is an essential skill. It allows the product manager to maintain clarity without rigidity. It also builds trust with operational teams, who often carry the burden of implementation. If those teams feel unheard or unconsidered, resistance builds, not because they dislike the product, but because they've seen too many top-down decisions fail in practice.

Respecting local context does not mean abandoning consistency. It means building systems that adapt intelligently to variability. It means accepting that some truths are universal, while others are site-specific. The product manager who understands these designs for durability—not just in what the product does, but in how it is introduced, supported, and sustained across complex, evolving environments.

CHAPTER 2

Product Lifecycle Management in Manufacturing Operations

Every product in a supply chain exists in motion, from idea to development, from testing to deployment, from maintenance to redesign. In manufacturing environments, especially within the energy sector, managing this lifecycle isn't just about process, it's about control. Not the kind of control that micromanages decisions or resists change, but the kind that maintains operational stability while allowing a product to evolve. In this space, product lifecycle management is about navigating tension, between what was designed, what is being delivered, and what is being used. And managing that tension requires structure, not slogans.

The lifecycle of a product in energy manufacturing isn't as linear as most models suggest. It doesn't follow a clean arc from development to launch to maturity. It loops. It pauses. It reopens when parts are recalled, when equipment fails, when regulations shift, or when performance in one region doesn't match what was tested in another. The lifecycle bends under pressure. And the product manager's job is to prevent it from breaking. That begins with scoping. Not just what the product is meant to do, but what it will require to survive where it will be used. A product built for modular integration in one plant may be too rigid for another. A sensor designed for high-heat applications may underperform in environments with constant dust exposure. These are not edge cases, they're common realities in manufacturing environments where equipment operates in imperfect conditions. This is why lifecycle scoping cannot be based only on design specs. It must include operational constraints, maintenance cycles, access to spare parts, and workforce capability.

Beyond scope, product lifecycle management involves planning for scale without assuming uniformity. The way a product performs in one region may not map neatly to another due to slight differences in supplier reliability, utility availability, or skill gaps within the workforce. This is why replicating success in industrial product rollout requires not just scaling the design, but scaling the support structure, documentation, local training, and onboarding systems around it. A good product with poor support infrastructure is still a weak product in practice. Managing the lifecycle means seeing the product as more than a physical asset. It includes everything the organization wraps around that asset to keep it alive.

One of the most difficult stages in the lifecycle to manage is the point where a product begins to show signs of performance drift but no one wants to call it failure. Maybe a defect rate increases. Maybe operators begin bypassing parts of the process. Maybe documentation starts falling out of sync with what's actually happening on the ground. These are early signals, and most organizations miss them because they only track issues after they become urgent. But in high-stakes environments like oil and gas, ignoring this stage creates long-term damage. It leads to recurring workarounds, emergency fixes, or quiet acceptance of inefficiency. A product manager who owns the full lifecycle watches for drift early. They build reporting channels that catch underperformance before it becomes normalized. And when necessary, they reintroduce discipline, not by blaming, but by recalibrating.

Managing the lifecycle also means understanding what happens after the product leaves the development team's hands. Who installs it? Who maintains it? Who troubleshoots it when things go wrong? In many manufacturing settings, these are not the same people. And yet, the way the product is documented, labeled, and designed often assumes a single user persona. That's a mistake. Real-world product usage is distributed across functions, and lifecycle planning must reflect that. Installation guides must make sense to technicians who've never seen the product before. Maintenance protocols must be designed for people working under time pressure. Interfaces must align with existing digital systems, not with an idealized workflow from the design team's imagination. These are not user experience enhancements, they're survival requirements. Because if the product becomes a burden at the point of use, it will be resisted, avoided, or quietly bypassed.

Sometimes lifecycle management involves difficult conversations. A product that no longer performs must be phased out. A strategy that once worked must be retired. A feature must be pulled if it creates more problems than it solves. These decisions are uncomfortable in environments that value reliability over disruption. But they're necessary. Good lifecycle management doesn't cling to legacy. It respects what's been built, but knows when to evolve, when to retire, and when to replace. And it manages that transition carefully, knowing that if people lose trust in how products are introduced or replaced, they will hesitate to adopt future solutions.

Another reality that product managers in this space must navigate is that lifecycle decisions are almost never made in isolation. They are bound by procurement cycles, contractual obligations, production calendars, and environmental audits. You cannot roll out a product redesign if procurement has already committed to a bulk order of the old model. You cannot update a process if regulators are auditing your current documentation. You cannot pull equipment out of rotation if production targets are already behind. These constraints are not excuses, they're real. Lifecycle planning that ignores them is destined to fail in execution. Which is why the best product managers in energy don't just own the product, they own the timing, the dependencies, and the relationships required to make lifecycle transitions smooth.

Some organizations treat product lifecycle as an afterthought, a downstream responsibility to be handled by operations once development is complete. But in energy manufacturing, this approach leads to fragmentation. Lifecycle management must be embedded from the start. The product roadmap should include launch, scale, support, monitoring, improvement, and retirement—not as vague intentions, but as specific, timed phases with clear accountability. This doesn't mean over-planning. It means anticipating complexity early so that it doesn't blindside the teams later. It means building in feedback loops that are both formal and informal. It means accepting that success is not just the product working as designed, but the organization being able to maintain that performance over time.

One of the least discussed aspects of lifecycle management in manufacturing is visibility, who sees what, and when. In many organizations, product teams are too far removed from what happens after a product enters production or gets handed off to operations. After the design files are signed off and specifications are approved, the product becomes someone else's problem. In theory, support tickets and usage reports should close that gap. But in practice, these feedback loops are often broken. Either the data never makes it back to the product team, or when it does, it arrives stripped of context; numbers without narrative, charts without the nuances behind them.

When visibility is fragmented, small problems linger too long. Patterns of underperformance go unnoticed. Workarounds become permanent. It's not that no one is paying attention, it's that the information is siloed or buried under other pressures. Operators may notice a part failing too frequently, but unless the maintenance logs are structured to highlight recurrence, that issue never escalates. Procurement may flag lead time challenges, but if those delays aren't explicitly tied to product-level decisions, they're treated as logistical hiccups rather than design flaws. The product continues to circulate in a form that no longer matches reality.

Closing that visibility gap requires more than data collection, it requires intentional relationships between product teams and the departments that live with the consequences of product decisions. These relationships can't be surface-level. They must be structured and sustained. Regular calls with field engineers. Debriefs after maintenance cycles. Site visits. Internal case studies that don't just celebrate success, but unpack failures without blame. Visibility is not passive. It has to be designed into the culture. And it has to be protected; especially when metrics are being used to justify resource allocation, cost reduction, or performance evaluations. Otherwise, feedback becomes distorted, and lifecycle decisions get made based on assumptions rather than operational truth.

Another factor that shapes the lifecycle is how early upstream teams, especially engineering and procurement, are brought into the process. Too often, product managers assume they own the planning phase exclusively, only looping in technical teams when they're ready to build or source. This delay in alignment leads to miscalculations. Engineering may surface compatibility issues late in the process, requiring expensive rework. Procurement may warn that a component spec is tied to a vendor with unstable supply history, but by then, the design is locked in. These misalignments are not caused by incompetence, they are structural. They happen because product teams don't always think of lifecycle planning as a multi-lane process. But that's what it is. And unless those lanes are running in parallel early enough, bottlenecks are inevitable.

When upstream teams are brought in late, they respond with caution, or resistance. And that resistance is not always unreasonable. In many cases, it reflects lessons learned from previous product rollouts that went poorly. Engineers may push back not because they dislike the new solution, but because they anticipate integration challenges that others can't see. Operators may hesitate because they know what it will take to retrain teams, update documentation, or secure compliance approvals. These insights should not be treated as objections, they are signals. Warnings. Early inputs that can be used to refine the rollout strategy. A product manager who interprets all resistance as inertia misses the opportunity to build smarter systems.

Resistance, in fact, is one of the clearest indicators that a product has touched something real. If no one pushes back, it may be because no one expects the product to affect their work. That's a sign of irrelevance, not success. Product managers must learn to interpret resistance, not with defensiveness, but with curiosity. What are people afraid of? What don't they trust? What has gone wrong in the past that they believe might happen again? These are not soft questions. They are strategic ones. And answering them strengthens the lifecycle, not just in planning, but in rollout, adoption, and long-term performance.

There's also the question of ownership. In many lifecycle discussions, it becomes unclear who is responsible once a product crosses a certain stage. The product manager led the development, but now operations is in charge of usage. Maintenance owns servicing. Quality owns auditing. Compliance owns documentation. IT owns the supporting systems. But when something breaks, who owns the response? When performance drifts, who recalibrates the process? When new functionality is needed, who initiates the change?

Without clear ownership at each phase of the lifecycle, accountability diffuses. And when accountability diffuses, performance erodes. Lifecycle management must define not just the timeline of a product, but the touchpoints, the triggers for action, and the roles responsible for each transition. This clarity allows teams to act quickly when needed—and to escalate appropriately when issues require cross-functional resolution. In environments where time, safety, and stability are always tense, that clarity is not a luxury. It's the only way products survive their full intended lifespan.

Lastly, lifecycle management in manufacturing operations must prepare for end-of-life planning, something most teams avoid until it's too late. A product does not become obsolete overnight. The warning signs show up early: decreasing performance, shrinking supplier options, regulatory misalignment, or simply a shift in market expectations. When end-of-life is not planned, organizations are forced into reactive scrambles; rushing redesigns, placing last-minute bulk orders, or scrambling to train teams on replacements. Planned obsolescence may sound cold, but in this environment, it's simply good governance. It allows transitions to be managed with time, resources, and communication, rather than panic.

The extended lifecycle of any product in the energy supply chain is full of opportunities, opportunities to reduce cost, improve safety, increase trust, and build operational intelligence. But those opportunities only reveal themselves to teams that treat the lifecycle as a living system—not a stage-gate formality. And they're only seized by product managers who are willing to stay close to the process long after the product has launched.

When product management is understood in this way, the work becomes deeper, but also more meaningful. It becomes about more than delivery. It becomes about durability. And in systems where failure is expensive, that durability is the most important product of all.

2.1 The Undervalued Power of Documentation

In most operational environments, documentation is seen as an afterthought, something needed for compliance audits, training manuals, or process handovers. It's rarely treated as a strategic part of the product lifecycle. But in supply chain-heavy sectors, especially energy and manufacturing, documentation plays a much bigger role. It determines how smoothly a product moves through each phase of its life and how quickly it recovers when something goes wrong.

When documentation is incomplete, outdated, or too abstract, the consequences show up immediately on the floor. Technicians hesitate. Teams interpret processes differently. Errors increase. Maintenance takes longer. And confidence in the product itself begins to erode. But when documentation is clear, field-tested, and actively maintained, it becomes more than a static reference, it becomes a live tool for operational intelligence.

Documentation in this space needs to be layered and adaptable. A single manual won't serve every function. Operators, quality inspectors, maintenance teams, and training coordinators all interact with the product differently. This means documentation should be modular, with role-specific guides that align with how people actually use, maintain, and troubleshoot the product in context. That includes creating:

- **Installation protocols** tailored to facility-specific constraints

- **Service checklists** aligned with available tools and shift schedules

- **Inspection procedures** designed for both internal QA teams and external auditors

- **Troubleshooting flows** that match the literacy and digital maturity of the users

It's not just about writing things down, it's about making those documents operationally useful. For example, a troubleshooting guide that assumes internet connectivity in a remote oilfield site won't help anyone. A digital manual that's only accessible on one platform may slow down urgent intervention. A schematic with ambiguous labeling might delay a repair that needs to happen in minutes, not hours. These are not minor inconveniences; they are productivity leaks.

Documentation also plays a huge role in handover moments; between shifts, between departments, and between locations. When new teams inherit a product mid-lifecycle without strong documentation, they inherit guesswork. That guesswork leads to small inefficiencies, which over time turn into recurring issues that no one fully understands or owns. A well-documented product, by contrast, reduces friction during these transitions. It creates continuity. It protects institutional knowledge from disappearing when someone leaves the team.

From a product management standpoint, documentation is also the clearest artifact of how decisions were made. It shows what was prioritized, what was excluded, what changed, and why. This becomes critical when evaluating performance years after deployment, especially if the original team is no longer in place. When lifecycle audits or redesign discussions happen, documentation becomes the link between memory and intent.

Unfortunately, in many product environments, documentation is outsourced too early or deprioritized entirely. It becomes a checklist item, delivered late and rarely updated. But in reality, it should be treated as a core deliverable of the product itself. It should be reviewed, field-tested, version-controlled, and actively distributed. Teams should be trained not just on the product, but on how to use the documentation that comes with it.

A culture of documentation is one of the clearest signs of a mature product organization. It signals that the team is building for continuity, not just launch. And in environments where the cost of miscommunication is high, that mindset is not just helpful, it's critical to long-term product success.

2.2 Where Lifecycle Planning Collides with Procurement Logic

One of the least visible, but most influential, forces shaping the product lifecycle is procurement. While the product manager may be responsible for defining what needs to be built, how it should function, and how long it should last, procurement often determines what actually gets delivered, how soon, and at what cost. When product decisions and procurement processes aren't aligned, lifecycle plans begin to drift before the product even reaches the floor.

Procurement teams operate under a different set of incentives. Their success is often measured in savings, contract efficiency, vendor management, and timely fulfillment. These are legitimate concerns, but they don't always align with lifecycle priorities like modularity, maintainability, or upgrade readiness. The result is a familiar scenario: a product designed with a flexible component strategy is altered during procurement to save costs by locking into a single vendor. Or a recommended part is substituted due to local availability, but the new option doesn't meet the durability or compliance profile the original design required.

This isn't always a matter of conflict. It's a matter of blind spots. Procurement is often brought into the process after critical design choices have already been made, or worse, they're asked to fill gaps with incomplete context. Product managers, meanwhile, are forced to adjust mid-lifecycle when procurement realities reshape the product's components, costs, or delivery timelines.

To avoid this, lifecycle planning must include procurement as an early and recurring partner, not just an endpoint in the supply chain. That means aligning timelines, sharing product roadmaps, and involving sourcing experts in component strategy conversations. It also means recognizing that procurement insights can add real value. A product manager might favor a highly specialized component for performance reasons, but if procurement data shows supply volatility or customs clearance risks, that decision needs to be re-evaluated before it introduces avoidable fragility.

There are also cases where procurement decisions impact the **post-launch phase** in subtle but significant ways. For example:

- A cheaper seal or gasket may pass initial QA but degrade faster, increasing field maintenance requests.

- A different packaging material might seem cost-efficient but add time and labor during installation.

- A local vendor may promise speed but lack the consistency needed to support scaled deployment.

These ripple effects land squarely in the product's operational phase, and by then, the original procurement rationale has often been forgotten. The product manager is left dealing with complaints, returns, or escalating support costs without direct control over the choices that caused them.

To prevent this disconnect, some organizations introduce procurement engineering roles or assign a dedicated sourcing partner to the product team. But even in leaner teams, alignment can be achieved through routine coordination, clear documentation of critical specifications, and mutual visibility into supplier performance data.

When lifecycle management respects procurement as a co-architect, not just a service function, the product benefits. It becomes easier to source reliably, scale predictably, and maintain quality over time. And when things do go wrong, it's easier to trace the cause and make decisions with the full picture in view.

2.3 Culture, Buy-In, and the Silent Saboteurs of Lifecycle Success

No matter how robust a lifecycle plan is on paper, its real performance depends on how it's received by the people who interact with the product every day. In industrial environments, where processes are deeply embedded and frontline teams are often under pressure; resistance to change doesn't always show up in meetings. It shows up in silence, in delays, in subtle workarounds, or in the quiet reversion to old tools and familiar processes. It's easy to interpret these behaviors as stubbornness or lack of initiative, but often they are signs of cultural misalignment between the product and the teams who are expected to adopt it.

Culture, in this context, is not about values painted on a wall. It's about trust. It's about historical memory. And it's about how change is experienced on the ground. Many frontline teams have lived through poorly executed rollouts. Systems that overpromised and underdelivered. Tools that were introduced with fanfare but removed months later due to performance issues. Processes that disrupted workflows without adding value. These experiences create skepticism, not because people fear change, but because they've seen it handled poorly before.

Product managers must recognize that culture is a real operational variable. It shapes how quickly feedback flows back, how thoroughly documentation is read, and how honestly problems are reported. A technician who believes a product is not truly supported won't bother logging every failure. An operator who feels blamed when a system underperforms will avoid offering suggestions. Over time, this kind of disengagement creates blind spots in the product lifecycle, making it harder to detect what's working, what's being ignored, and what's quietly failing.

This is why stakeholder engagement must be continuous, not just at rollout. Teams need to see that their feedback leads to changes. That issues raised are acknowledged, not deflected. That leadership is aligned not just in words but in response times and resource allocation. Building this trust takes time, but it pays off. When frontline teams feel heard and respected, they become partners in improving the product. They surface small issues before they become big ones. They test fixes more willingly. They own outcomes.

A practical approach to building buy-in includes:

- Involving teams in early testing phases, even if only in feedback roles

- Using site champions or experienced operators as peer advocates during rollout

- Acknowledging local adaptations instead of forcing uniformity from day one

- Returning regularly for follow-ups, not just data collection

Lifecycle management that ignores these soft factors often creates avoidable friction. Resistance builds quietly, but once entrenched, it takes serious effort to reverse. And in energy and manufacturing contexts, where turnover is low and institutional memory runs deep—early missteps can shape perceptions of a product for years.

In contrast, when culture is accounted for, adoption becomes smoother. Teams feel invested in the product's success. They report bugs not as complaints, but as contributions. They take pride in maintaining uptime, not just because it's their job, but because they had a voice in the tools and systems supporting them.

Lifecycle planning must, therefore, extend beyond the product itself. It must include the people who keep the product alive. Their buy-in is not a bonus, it's a condition for long-term success.

2.4 Designing for Resilience: Modularity and the Lifecycle Beyond Launch

A product's value isn't just determined by how well it performs today; it's defined by how well it holds up when conditions change. In energy and manufacturing, conditions always change. Demand fluctuates. Regulations evolve. Technologies improve. Supplier networks shift. And yet, many product decisions are still made with a fixed mindset, assuming stability in a world that guarantees volatility. This is where resilience becomes a defining trait of modern product lifecycle management.

Resilience doesn't just mean durability. It means adaptability. It means designing products, systems, and documentation in ways that make them easier to upgrade, reconfigure, or extend without starting from scratch. In practical terms, that means building with modularity in mind—not just for mechanical systems, but for digital components, process logic, and support infrastructure as well.

Modularity allows organizations to react quickly when one part of the system needs to evolve. A modular component can be swapped out without revalidating the entire product. A modular software update can be pushed to specific functions without destabilizing the full platform. A modular training model allows new personnel to onboard without requiring a complete overhaul of the existing system. These efficiencies matter. They reduce downtime. They limit dependency. They help teams maintain control in moments of uncertainty.

Building modularity into the product lifecycle also future-proofs design decisions. For example:

- **Choosing components with multiple sourcing options** reduces vendor lock-in and improves supply chain flexibility.

- **Standardizing interfaces** allows future tools or updates to integrate without redesign.

- **Separating core functionality from user-specific configurations** helps tailor the product to different contexts without duplicating effort.

- **Version-controlling documentation and change logs** makes it easier to trace, audit, and revise over time.

These strategies aren't glamorous, but they are essential in sectors where product lifecycles span years—or decades. They allow the product to evolve without collapsing under the weight of its original design assumptions. They also reduce technical debt, improve maintainability, and support scalability across regions, use cases, and market conditions.

Resilience also involves the way a product retires. A resilient product lifecycle includes end-of-life protocols that minimize disruption. It includes phase-out plans, cross-training, legacy system support, and well-timed procurement triggers. The product manager who plans for a product's eventual obsolescence is not being negative, they are being responsible.

Because in high-stakes supply chains, nothing ends neatly unless it was planned that way.

Too often, resilience is framed as a reactive strategy; something activated only in response to crisis. But in lifecycle management, resilience must be baked in from the beginning. It should be visible in design choices, process workflows, sourcing strategies, and documentation practices. It should be part of every conversation about cost, risk, and long-term value.

When a product is designed with resilience in mind, it doesn't just meet its goals; it keeps meeting them even as the world around it changes. And in industries built on uptime, safety, and continuity, that is what defines excellence.

CHAPTER 3

Designing for Efficiency: Strategic Alignment in Supply Chains

Efficiency isn't just a metric, it's a mindset. In the context of product management within the supply chain, especially in energy and manufacturing, efficiency has less to do with moving faster and more to do with moving intelligently. Speed, without alignment, creates waste. Coordination without strategy produces friction. What matters isn't just how quickly a product moves from development to delivery, but whether that movement happens with structural clarity, cross-functional cooperation, and operational balance.

At its core, efficiency in supply chain-aligned product management is about reduction. Reducing friction. Reducing handoff errors. Reducing downtime. Reducing complexity without sacrificing control. But that reduction doesn't happen through shortcuts. It happens through systems design, through aligning the product's trajectory with the realities of how supply chains operate and where they break down.

Many inefficiencies in product delivery are not caused by poor planning, but by poor timing. A product is technically ready, but procurement has not secured key components. Engineering has completed testing, but the logistics network isn't prepared for scale. A tool is deployed, but the infrastructure to support it hasn't caught up. These moments create dead space, windows where momentum slows, costs rise, and team confidence weakens. They're not always dramatic failures, but over time, they create a drain on trust, resources, and execution capability. Strategic alignment prevents these gaps, not by forcing everyone into the same rhythm, but by designing product lifecycles around shared points of convergence.

To design for efficiency, the product manager must act as a coordinator of cadences. Different teams work at different speeds, under different pressures. Supply teams are watching shipping delays and customs regulations. Engineering teams are chasing tolerances and approval checklists. Operations teams are managing labor, uptime, and resource planning. Each group has valid priorities, but they don't always translate cleanly across functions. What looks like a quick pivot in product design might represent six weeks of rework for procurement. What seems like a harmless vendor change might require re-certification for safety teams. The role of the product manager is to align those timelines, not by slowing everything down, but by planning the product's path with respect to these realities from the beginning.

This requires more than status meetings. It requires visibility. Product managers must understand the lead time behavior of their supply chain. They need to know how upstream constraints will affect downstream activity. They must account for seasonal fluctuations, labor cycles, fiscal year ends, and contract renewal periods. Efficiency is not about pushing harder, it's about reducing the surprises that slow everyone down.

Strategic alignment also means resisting the temptation to treat efficiency as a local optimization exercise. Too many product teams fall into the trap of optimizing one part of the system without considering its impact on the whole. A feature is introduced that speeds up onboarding, but increases complexity for the support team. A tool is added to improve inspection accuracy, but doubles the workload of field technicians. A component is replaced to improve durability, but causes new delays due to limited vendor availability. These are not bad decisions, they're incomplete ones. Designing for efficiency requires systemic thinking. It requires asking not just "does this make our work faster?" but "does this make the system better?"

True efficiency in supply chain-oriented product environments is often invisible. When done right, things just flow. Deliveries show up when they're supposed to. Teams know what they're building, why it matters, and when to expect the next phase. Systems communicate without constant escalation. Meetings become shorter, because people are aligned before they arrive. This kind of efficiency isn't dramatic, but it is deeply felt. And when it disappears, everything slows down.

One of the keys to maintaining this flow is role clarity. Efficiency doesn't mean fewer people, it means fewer questions about who owns what. When product managers define roles clearly, teams waste less time negotiating responsibility. Escalations become rare, not because problems don't happen, but because the pathway to resolution is known. Strategic alignment reduces the overhead required to manage routine work. That mental and procedural clarity frees up bandwidth for innovation, problem-solving, and improvement; activities that often get buried under the noise of misalignment.

Designing for efficiency also means knowing when to say no. Every supply chain has a threshold. Every team has a capacity limit. Every rollout has risk. When product managers pursue new features, configurations, or extensions without respect for these limits, efficiency begins to fracture. A product may technically "launch," but if it overwhelms the teams tasked with sustaining it, it's not a win. It's a short-term illusion of progress, followed by long-term drag.

This is why product managers in the energy sector must develop an internal filter, a sense of when to push for more and when to refine what already exists. That filter comes from experience, but it's shaped by paying attention to the lagging signals of strain: increasing support tickets, repeated errors in deployment, delayed updates, growing silence from frontline teams. These aren't just operational issues. They're indicators that alignment has slipped. And if efficiency is the goal, these signals must be addressed, not buried under launch milestones or vanity metrics.

Efficiency also thrives in environments with healthy friction, the kind where different teams challenge each other constructively. Procurement should pressure design to justify cost. Operations should push product teams to simplify. Legal and compliance should probe for risks that others overlook. When these dynamics are encouraged, not silenced, they produce sharper products and stronger processes. Strategic alignment doesn't mean avoiding disagreement. It means managing it well.

One of the least visible barriers to efficiency in supply chain-aligned product management is indecision. Not the dramatic kind where teams openly clash over a direction, but the quieter kind, where approval is delayed, alignment isn't reached, or small decisions keep slipping off the agenda. In complex systems, these delays compound. A three-day pause in vendor selection causes a knock-on delay in onboarding, which pushes out pilot testing, which then collides with a regulatory submission window, which finally forces a reactive shift in go-to-market timing. None of these issues on their own seem significant, but together, they erode delivery confidence and strain team morale.

The irony is that in energy and manufacturing, teams often pride themselves on being decisive in crisis, but tolerate hesitation in planning. They respond quickly when systems go down, when production halts, when something breaks. But upstream, when product strategy decisions need to be locked in or rollout options need executive sign-off, the pace slows down. Meetings are rescheduled. Ownership is unclear. Momentum fades. This disconnect; fast under pressure, slow under planning, undermines efficiency at its root.

The product manager's responsibility is to guard against this drift. Not by pushing relentlessly, but by building systems that keep decision-making visible. Decisions that are not made must be tracked with the same rigor as decisions that are. Open items must be named, not buried under updates. Teams must be encouraged to surface dependencies early, to flag unresolved debates, to make trade-offs explicit rather than implied. In high-stakes environments, deferred decisions often feel safer. But in supply chain-driven systems, time is not neutral. Every delay has a cost, even if that cost is hard to measure in the moment.

Trade-offs are inevitable in any product effort, but in energy, those trade-offs are structural. Do you prioritize standardization or local customization? Do you design for perfect fit or future flexibility? Do you reduce cost now or improve serviceability later? These choices cannot be eliminated. What matters is how they are managed, and whether they're surfaced before they become operational constraints.

Efficiency is not found in perfect outcomes. It's found in the ability to respond when plans shift. When a supplier underperforms, is there a pre-approved backup? When a critical component fails inspection, does the product design allow for substitution without weeks of reengineering? When new environmental standards are introduced, is there a clear path to adapt documentation, processes, and support systems? These questions are not about agility in the abstract. They are about responsiveness under pressure, and responsiveness depends on the design of the system, not just the speed of the team.

Another silent contributor to inefficiency is misaligned definitions of success. One department measures efficiency by reducing cost per unit. Another values reduced downtime. A third is tracking adoption rates. None of these are wrong, but if they aren't harmonized, they lead to contradictory decisions. A product change made to reduce per-unit cost might inadvertently increase install time, disrupting throughput. A feature added to improve adoption might introduce complexity that the quality team struggles to validate. Alignment doesn't mean forcing one metric across all teams, it means making the trade-offs between metrics visible and agreed upon.

There's also a cost to pretending complexity doesn't exist. Product managers sometimes fall into the trap of oversimplifying supply chain dynamics when presenting to leadership—painting a picture that suggests everything is under control. While this may preserve short-term confidence, it often delays hard conversations about risk, resource gaps, and systemic inefficiencies. Efficiency is not the absence of problems, it is the ability to surface them early and respond without panic. That ability is built on a culture of operational honesty, not theatrical calm.

True alignment also demands that strategy is not confused with communication. A team can be well-informed and still misaligned. Regular updates, clear documentation, and visible dashboards are important, but they do not guarantee shared intent. Product managers must check not just whether stakeholders have been informed, but whether they are operating from the same assumptions. A logistics team operating under outdated cost expectations can make decisions that contradict the current product direction. A regional operations team unaware of an upcoming system integration might block features out of caution, not malice. Misalignment isn't always caused by conflict. Often, it's just incomplete context.

In energy and manufacturing, the cost of misalignment is rarely immediate. It shows up months later, in missed targets, surprise overruns, slow adoption, or unnecessary firefighting. That delay makes it dangerous, because by the time the symptoms appear, the original cause has been forgotten. Designing for efficiency means building not just processes, but memory, ways to trace cause and effect, to link early choices with later outcomes. That's what allows teams to improve, not just repeat.

3.1 The Role of System Visibility in Operational Efficiency

In energy and manufacturing operations, most inefficiencies don't happen because teams aren't working—they happen because teams are working in the dark. The product manager may have a clean roadmap, the procurement team may have vendor timelines, and operations may have their shift targets, but if no one can see beyond their task into the broader system, efficiency collapses. Visibility isn't just about dashboards or reporting tools, it's about how clearly people understand the state of the system and the impact of their decisions on others downstream.

Without visibility, teams optimize for their silo. Procurement secures the fastest available part, not realizing it will require a redesign of an adjacent component. Engineering updates specs without informing the documentation team, who publish outdated manuals. A delay in testing is not flagged until the day of a scheduled deployment, forcing teams to scramble to reschedule logistics, personnel, and site access. In each case, the inefficiency is not the result of bad intent or poor performance, it's the result of uncoordinated work done under conditions of partial awareness.

What makes this especially dangerous in supply chain-aligned environments is that the product is often moving through systems with interdependent timelines. One delay quietly compounds another. When no one sees the full picture, no one owns the delay. People react to symptoms, not causes. This leads to chronic firefighting, strained relationships between teams, and a creeping loss of confidence in the product's delivery system. Once confidence erodes, collaboration becomes defensive. Teams protect themselves from blame rather than contribute openly to shared progress.

Visibility solves this—but not automatically. Tools alone do not create alignment. Many organizations deploy expensive systems for tracking timelines, reporting progress, and logging performance, only to find that the data isn't used or trusted. True visibility is not about pushing more information—it's about surfacing the right information in the right format for the people who need to act on it. That might mean visual trackers for inventory in regional warehouses. It might mean maintenance alerts based on machine learning models tied to field conditions. It might mean something as basic as a shared log of late-stage product changes; updated daily, accessible to all, and reviewed consistently in cross-functional check-ins.

For visibility to create efficiency, it must become part of the daily operational rhythm. That means designing meetings around decision points, not just updates. It means removing lag between problem detection and escalation. It means pushing status awareness down to the front lines, not locking it behind management reporting cycles. Most importantly, it means being honest about what isn't working. Too often, visibility is curated for presentation rather than shared for action. The result is a false sense of progress, masking underlying system stress that will eventually surface in the form of missed deadlines or budget overruns.

Product managers must be the custodians of visibility. They must champion radical clarity, not to shame teams, but to align them. They must fight for accurate timelines, traceable decisions, and consistent reporting not because those things look good on slides, but because they allow everyone to see what matters: where the product is, what it needs, and who is responsible for what happens next.

Without that kind of visibility, efficiency becomes a guessing game. But when visibility is designed into the flow of work, efficiency becomes the natural outcome, because people are no longer managing assumptions. They're managing reality.

3.2 The Hidden Drain of Context Switching on Execution

Efficiency often gets measured in deliverables, what gets completed, what moves forward, what goes live. But what's harder to track, and often far more damaging, is what gets delayed or degraded due to fragmented focus. In cross-functional product environments, especially those spanning procurement, manufacturing, operations, and compliance, teams are constantly forced to split attention. They jump between competing priorities, answer to multiple stakeholders, and juggle legacy tasks while onboarding new initiatives. On paper, everything is moving. In reality, energy is leaking everywhere.

Context switching is not just a cognitive issue, it's a structural one. Every time a product team has to shift from debugging a vendor delay to resolving a spec miscommunication or preparing a board update, there is a cost. That cost doesn't always appear in reports. It appears in dropped context, missed details, duplicated effort, and vague follow-ups that go nowhere. It shows up when a task is "in progress" for weeks because no one has had the space to give it their full attention. It shows up in the form of meetings where everyone is present but no one is truly focused. It shows up in rising burnout and falling initiative.

In energy-sector environments where systems are complex and stakes are high, the consequences of fragmented attention are amplified. A missed detail in a compliance update could delay certification. A misaligned schedule for asset delivery could cause a cascading delay across multiple sites. A change request that isn't followed through because the team's attention shifted elsewhere can trigger operational confusion at the worst possible time.

Product managers, especially those working across supply chains, need to design against this drain. That means creating clarity not just around what needs to be done, but when, by whom, and in what order. It means resisting the urge to overload the roadmap with parallel initiatives that all sound important but compete for the same operational bandwidth. It means sequencing projects intentionally, protecting deep work time for teams that need it, and pushing back when too many efforts risk crowding each other out.

One of the simplest but most powerful efficiency levels is structured focus. This can look like organizing delivery cycles around capacity, not just urgency. It can involve rotating task ownership to prevent single points of overload. It might require redesigning escalation paths to avoid routing every issue through the same few decision-makers. These are not productivity hacks; they're lifecycle strategies. Because a fragmented product team cannot deliver an aligned, efficient supply chain experience.

Efficiency doesn't just break when something is late. It breaks when people are too busy to notice what's going wrong. When no one has the mental space to ask "is this still the right direction?" When tasks become automatic responses instead of deliberate moves. In these moments, the product loses its rhythm. And even small inefficiencies start to feel like fatigue.

The real work of designing for efficiency is not in moving faster. It's in reducing unnecessary motion. It's in building alignment that lasts past kickoff meetings. It's in honoring the limited attention of teams by giving them what they need: clarity, priority, and the time to execute without being pulled in five directions at once.

When that happens, when focus is respected as a resource, efficiency becomes more than a performance goal. It becomes a working condition. And in a supply chain world built on complexity, that is what gives products their real chance to succeed.

CHAPTER 4

AI-Powered Optimization in Energy Product Management

Artificial intelligence is no longer a forward-looking concept in energy systems, it's a functional tool that has already reshaped the way supply chains, maintenance systems, and operational workflows are being run. Yet, for many organizations, the promise of AI still feels distant. The hype is loud, but implementation is messy. Models are built, but not used. Dashboards exist, but are ignored. Predictions are accurate, but not trusted. The problem isn't capability. It's integration. The real challenge of AI in product management is not building smarter tools, it's making them work within existing systems without overwhelming the people who rely on them.

In energy operations, the stakes are high. One decision made with incomplete data can result in asset downtime, safety risks, or millions in lost revenue. AI offers the promise of faster insights, predictive capabilities, and automation, but only if those outputs are delivered in ways that can be acted on, under pressure, with confidence. This means the role of the product manager is not just to advocate for AI, but to curate it. To translate complex models into usable systems. To build workflows around prediction, not in place of process, but in support of it.

At its best, AI turns reaction into prevention. Maintenance schedules that used to be based on fixed intervals or reactive repairs can now be shaped by machine learning models that analyze equipment wear, pressure cycles, vibration signatures, and temperature trends. These systems don't guess—they learn. They flag anomalies early, recommend interventions before failure, and prioritize assets based on risk, usage, or cost impact. But that potential only becomes real when the data sources are clean, the models are trained with context, and the operational team trusts the output enough to act on it.

That trust takes work to build. Field teams are not impressed by theoretical accuracy. They care about whether a flagged alert actually corresponds to a problem they can find. They care whether the tool understands the rhythm of their facility, or whether it's offering generalized advice that feels detached from reality. When AI models are introduced without grounding in site-specific behavior, they get tuned out. When recommendations appear without transparency, teams fall back to intuition. And when failures occur despite predictive systems being in place, confidence drops sharply. This is not an argument against AI, it's a call for intelligent implementation.

Product managers navigating AI integration must begin with use cases, not algorithms. What is the operational problem we're solving? What decision currently takes too long, happens too late, or relies too much on gut instinct? In supply chain-heavy environments, that list is long. Inventory forecasting, demand planning, routing optimization, quality inspection, maintenance scheduling, all of these are ripe for improvement. But if everything is a priority, nothing gets traction. The product manager must select early wins carefully: systems where the data is ready, the feedback loop is tight, and the users are close enough to the problem to validate improvements.

This work also involves rethinking how intelligence is distributed. In the past, data analytics was a back-office function. Reports were generated, analyzed, and then passed downstream. But AI changes that flow. It allows intelligence to sit at the edge, on the line, in the truck, in the terminal. Technicians can receive real-time alerts. Drivers can get route recommendations updated based on weather or congestion. Site managers can visualize supply risks and model decisions before committing to them. This democratization of insight is powerful, but only if teams are trained to interpret it, and only if the interfaces are designed with usability in mind.

AI-powered tools must compete with habits. In many organizations, workflows have evolved through years of manual expertise. Teams know what to expect from a system, even if it's inefficient. When a predictive tool is introduced, it disrupts that rhythm. This disruption can be positive, but it must be acknowledged. Change management is not a soft issue, it is a performance variable. If the product manager doesn't plan for resistance, adoption will stall. If they don't build feedback channels, the AI system will evolve in isolation, making outputs less accurate over time. If they don't communicate the limits of the model, trust will be lost the first time it fails.

The product lifecycle also changes under AI. Products must now be managed not just in terms of components and documentation, but in terms of models, data pipelines, sensor integrity, and model drift. A product that includes an AI system must be monitored, retrained, and recalibrated over time. It must be designed to learn, but also to be corrected. The product manager must plan for these cycles, staff them, and budget for them. AI doesn't reduce the need for oversight. It shifts that oversight into new domains; data quality, system integration, and user trust.

None of this means AI is too complex to implement. It simply means that AI maturity takes more than a pilot program or a vendor partnership. It takes operational awareness, lifecycle planning, and a clear strategy for how intelligence will shape decisions. Done well, AI doesn't replace people, it makes them faster, clearer, and more consistent. It doesn't eliminate risk, it brings risk into focus earlier. It doesn't guarantee outcomes but it improves the conditions under which outcomes are achieved.

In high-pressure supply chains, that improvement matters. The ability to detect, decide, and act faster than before is a competitive edge. It protects uptime. It reduces waste. It prevents small problems from becoming systemic failures. AI, when managed well, becomes a quiet layer of foresight, working in the background, surfacing signals, and helping teams make smarter moves.

But the credit for success will not go to the algorithm. It will go to the product leaders who made it usable. Who translated potential into performance. Who built trust, built systems, and stayed close enough to the field to know when the system was actually working.

One of the most underestimated barriers to AI adoption is infrastructure readiness. It's easy to talk about real-time analytics, predictive alerts, and automated decision-making. It's harder to implement these capabilities in facilities where network connectivity is spotty, hardware varies across sites, and data logging is inconsistent at best. In many energy operations, especially those spread across rural, offshore, or legacy-built environments; digital maturity is uneven. Some locations are sensor-rich and data-literate; others still rely on paper logs, manual reporting, and operator intuition. This fragmentation isn't a reason to delay AI, it's a reason to design it differently.

To deliver AI-powered optimization in these conditions, product managers must make architecture choices that respect operational variance. That might mean hybrid systems that store and process data locally when connectivity is limited, then sync when online. It might mean simplifying the data schema to match what teams can realistically collect and maintain. It might even mean building models that can learn from small, imperfect datasets rather than waiting for the ideal. Perfection is not the goal—progress is. And sometimes, the best way to scale intelligence is to build it for constraint, not luxury.

But even when infrastructure is available, another challenge arises: interpretability. AI, in its rawest form, is often a black box. It produces an answer but not an explanation. For a data science team, this might be acceptable. For a field technician deciding whether to shut down a pump, it's not. If an AI system flags a fault, the team needs to understand why. Was it a temperature anomaly? A vibration spike? A historical pattern? Without clarity, the alert becomes noise, and eventually, noise becomes ignored. Interpretability is not a nice-to-have, it's an adoption requirement. And the responsibility for making AI interpretable doesn't fall on the model alone. It falls on the product team to design interfaces, explain logic, and build user trust in how the system "thinks."

This need for clarity becomes even more urgent when AI starts triggering action. A suggestion is one thing, a command is another. When systems begin to automate decisions, rerouting supply, adjusting performance parameters, or issuing maintenance orders, they cross into operational territory where every action has a cost. If the AI gets it wrong, who is accountable? If it triggers the wrong outcome, how quickly can it be reversed? The product manager must anticipate these risks and build safeguards; manual overrides, audit logs, layered permissions. Intelligence must never remove responsibility. It must support it.

Another dynamic that product teams often face is the scaling problem. An AI model might work well in a controlled pilot; one site, one system, one set of users. But once scaled to multiple locations, variations emerge. Equipment is slightly different. Operators use the tool in unexpected ways. Data cleanliness drops. Edge conditions become more frequent. The model begins to lose precision, and trust begins to erode. This is where lifecycle thinking reenters the picture. AI is not a "deploy and forget" solution. It needs maintenance, retraining, recalibration. Just like a machine needs oil changes and inspections, an AI model needs supervision. The product manager must plan for that care—not as a technical afterthought, but as part of the long-term operational structure.

There's also the issue of alignment. In many organizations, AI implementation is siloed. A data science team builds something useful, but it never connects to product strategy or user workflow. The result is a powerful tool that no one uses, not because it doesn't work, but because it wasn't built into the rhythm of the real operation. To change this, product managers must bring AI into the core of their planning. They must work with data teams early, not to dictate models, but to anchor priorities. What decisions do users need help making? What processes are time-sensitive and error-prone? What insights would change the way work gets done, not just how it gets reported?

These questions help shift AI from an experimental layer to a foundational one. And when that shift happens, the value becomes measurable. Decision time shortens. Asset life increases. Inventory gets leaner. Quality becomes more consistent. And every team downstream benefits, not because they learned how AI works, but because the product team made AI work for them.

This is what real AI optimization looks like in energy systems, not sci-fi automation or algorithm obsession, but grounded, context-driven application that improves the work already being done. It's not just about replacing manual steps. It's about enhancing operational foresight, giving teams earlier signals, clearer choices, and better control. And it's about doing so in ways that respect the rhythm, risk, and realities of the environments where these tools must live.

If AI is to truly reshape product management in supply chain systems, it must move beyond pilots and slide decks. It must become embedded; technically, culturally, and strategically. That only happens when product managers stay close to the system, close to the users, and close to the data. It's not just about what the model knows. It's about whether the system helps people make better decisions at the moments they matter most.

That's the promise of AI. And that's the job.

4.1 Choosing the Right Use Cases: Where AI Actually Delivers Value

The fastest way to stall an AI initiative is to apply it in the wrong place. In energy and manufacturing systems, where operations are often capital-intensive, regulated, and deeply interdependent, even good ideas can backfire if they're introduced in the wrong sequence, at the wrong scale, or in the wrong domain. That's why AI implementation must begin not with what's possible, but with what's necessary. The most successful applications of AI in supply chain-aligned product environments start with use cases where operational pain is high, data exists in usable form, and improvement is measurable. That sweet spot is what makes or breaks early momentum.

Too often, teams default to flashy or high-level projects; predicting market demand across multiple countries, automating entire asset inspection lifecycles, or attempting real-time optimization of inventory flow across all warehouses. These are noble goals, but they're complex, messy, and highly dependent on data maturity that most organizations haven't achieved. The better approach is to start with focused use cases that are close to the ground: identifying shipment delays based on weather and route data; predicting part failure in a specific model of compressor; optimizing fuel usage for a defined type of vehicle on a specific route. These are narrow enough to execute, but impactful enough to prove value.

The best early use cases for AI share a few traits:

- **They support high-volume, repeatable decisions** that are currently made with guesswork or experience.

- **They have clear economic impact** when improved, either through savings, uptime, or reduced rework.

- **They can be isolated and measured** without requiring major system-wide rearchitecture.

- **They align with workflows that are already in place**, so the insight can be absorbed without disrupting the rhythm of work.

For example, in a refinery where thousands of components must be monitored, applying AI to all equipment simultaneously is overwhelming. But applying anomaly detection to a single pump category with a known failure profile can generate early wins. Similarly, trying to automate entire inspection checklists using AI vision may be ambitious. But using computer vision to flag missing safety gear or structural anomalies in scaffolding photos may offer quick, meaningful traction.

Product managers must work closely with operators, engineers, and asset managers to surface these kinds of use cases, not just by asking "Where can AI help?" but by observing where decisions are most fragile, where data is already being captured, and where errors tend to repeat. These are the places where AI can create leverage, without overwhelming the system or alienating the people who run it.

And once those initial use cases succeed, they create the runway for more. Trust grows. Funding increases. Teams begin to ask for the tools, rather than resist them. And that shift, from push to pull—is the moment AI stops being a novelty and becomes part of how the organization thinks.

4.2 Supporting Data Quality Without Becoming a Data Scientist

Every AI system is only as good as the data that feeds it. But in most energy and supply chain organizations, the product manager is not the person writing the data pipeline or engineering the database. Still, the success of any AI-driven product feature depends on whether the right data is being collected, structured, cleaned, and used consistently. That means product managers need to sit close enough to the data to guide priorities, but not so close that they're micromanaging data teams. This balance is subtle, but essential.

Many organizations treat "data" as a solved problem once sensors are installed or once software starts logging events. But in reality, raw data is often incomplete, mislabeled, stored in inconsistent formats, or captured without the context needed to interpret it. For example, vibration data from a pump might be collected every hour, but if it isn't tagged with operating load, ambient temperature, or usage cycles, it may mislead the model into seeing noise as signal. Similarly, supply chain data might capture delivery times, but not the reasons behind delays. The result is a surface-level understanding that produces shallow insights.

Product managers can't fix these issues by themselves. But they can ask the right questions:

- Where is this data coming from?
- Is it complete? Does it represent real behavior?
- Are there known gaps or inconsistencies?
- What does the team using this data need to trust it?

These questions push the organization toward data maturity, not by demanding technical perfection, but by framing the work in terms of product impact. When product managers embed data quality into backlog grooming, sprint planning, or postmortem reviews, they send a signal: data isn't just a technical asset, it's product dependent.

One of the most impactful things a product manager can do is help prioritize which data matters. Not all fields in a database need to be cleaned. Not every log file needs to be perfect. But the data that powers prediction, triggers alerts, or feeds automated decisions, those must be protected. That means investing in monitoring for anomalies, versioning for changes, and metadata to document meaning.

Data quality also involves advocacy. Often, the teams who generate or steward the data are not the same ones who use it. Product managers must bridge that gap, helping field teams understand why a new logging procedure is important, or helping data teams understand how missing values affect real-world decisions. This is part of stakeholder management. And it's what separates AI that lives in a lab from AI that lives in operations.

Finally, product managers must plan for decay. Just like physical systems wear down, data systems drift. Sensors go offline. Usage patterns change. Labels lose relevance. AI models built on yesterday's assumptions begin to perform worse, not because they're broken, but because the world moved. Product teams must work with data and engineering teams to establish revalidation cycles, freshness checks, and performance audits. That way, they're not caught off guard when performance dips, and they're not dependent on user complaints to discover that something is wrong.

Supporting data quality isn't glamorous work. It doesn't generate headlines or earn immediate praise. But it is the foundation of every AI system worth building. And when product managers do it well, they make the entire system more intelligent, not by adding features, but by protecting the integrity of the facts those features rely on.

4.3 Governing AI Systems: Performance, Accountability, and Lifecycle Discipline

Once an AI-powered feature goes live, the real work begins. Unlike static product features, AI systems are living systems, they interact with the environment, learn from patterns, and evolve over time. This makes them powerful, but also fragile. Without clear governance, AI systems degrade quietly. A model that once predicted maintenance needs with 90% accuracy may begin to drift, returning false positives or missing failures altogether. A routing algorithm trained on historical fuel prices may become unreliable in volatile markets. A quality scoring model built on one region's production behavior may not translate to another. These shifts often happen slowly, but they carry steep consequences when left unchecked.

Product managers cannot rely on data scientists alone to manage this. AI governance is a cross-functional responsibility, and it begins with visibility. Every AI-enabled feature in the product stack should be tied to a defined set of performance indicators; tracked not just during testing, but in active use. If a predictive maintenance feature begins recommending unnecessary work orders, that's a governance issue. If a recommendation engine starts suggesting unreliable vendors based on outdated supplier metrics, that's a governance issue. These aren't just technical glitches, they're product failures. And the longer they go unnoticed, the more damage they do to user trust.

One way to prevent this is to define the AI lifecycle the same way we define physical or software lifecycles. That means including retraining schedules, update plans, and model performance review points into the broader product roadmap. Just as a sensor might be replaced after a year of use, a model may need to be retrained quarterly. Just as firmware might need version control, so do AI configurations. And just as safety-critical features require audit trails, so should decisions influenced by AI.

Another layer of governance is escalation. If a user disagrees with an AI suggestion, especially one tied to safety, compliance, or large capital decisions, what happens? Is there a way to override the system? Can that override be reviewed? Logged? Learned from? Too many AI deployments assume the system will be obeyed. But in real environments, especially high-trust technical domains like energy, operators still need authority. AI must advise, not dictate. And when its advice is wrong, the system should be capable of improving from that feedback.

Regulatory pressure will only make this more important. As AI becomes more embedded in physical systems; from inspection tools to autonomous field vehicles, governance is no longer a back-office task. It's a requirement. Governments, clients, insurers, and internal audit teams will want proof that the AI being used to make decisions is being monitored, managed, and improved. Product managers must prepare for this, not as a future problem, but as a current necessity.

Doing this well creates a virtuous cycle. When governance is in place, AI systems perform more reliably. When performance is reliable, trust grows. When trust grows, adoption spreads. And when adoption spreads, the data improves; feeding the system and strengthening its value over time. But that only happens when product teams treat AI not as a feature, but as an ongoing relationship, one that must be supported, questioned, and maintained.

AI is not magic. It's math, data, systems, and assumptions; woven together to help people make better decisions. And like any part of a product system, it must be managed with care. The more it's trusted, the more carefully it must be governed. Because in the end, what makes AI valuable isn't its ability to predict the future, it's its ability to improve the present, without breaking what already works.

CHAPTER 5

Intelligent Quality Control and Assurance Models

In the high-pressure world of energy and manufacturing, quality is not just a department, it's a promise. A product that fails quality expectations doesn't just reflect poorly on the team behind it; it exposes the entire supply chain to risk. That risk may be reputational, regulatory, environmental, or financial, but in all cases, it's expensive. And yet, for too long, quality assurance has been treated as a checkpoint, something that happens after the fact, once production is complete or a delivery is made. In reality, quality is not something you test for. It's something you build for. And intelligent quality control begins at the design phase, not the final stage.

For product managers, this means rethinking the role of quality entirely. Instead of seeing it as the responsibility of the QA team, it must be integrated into the product lifecycle, embedded into the supply chain, and enforced through systems that are proactive, not reactive. In traditional settings, quality checks often rely on sampling, physical inspections, and historical knowledge. But as operations scale and complexity increases, these methods can no longer keep up. Modern supply chains require quality systems that are faster, smarter, and predictive, not just reactive to what has already gone wrong.

This is where intelligent quality control comes in, not just through automation, but through structure. A quality model should not only detect defects, but also identify patterns. It should highlight systemic issues, reveal weak points in training, equipment, or sourcing, and offer feedback that informs both upstream design decisions and downstream service protocols. This doesn't require cutting-edge AI on day one. What it requires is clarity: What does quality mean for this product, in this context? What are we trying to protect? And what failure patterns do we refuse to normalize?

In energy operations, quality is often directly tied to safety. A subpar weld, a misaligned valve, a faulty sensor, each of these can escalate into system failures, shutdowns, or even catastrophic events. The tolerance for error is low, and the cost of rework is high. For the product manager, this means decisions must be made with a quality-first mindset. Not every enhancement is worth the additional risk. Not every redesign should prioritize speed. Product managers must balance innovation with consistency, and novelty with proven reliability. The best product teams are not those who ship the fastest, they are the ones who reduce the number of things that need to be fixed later.

Another dimension of modern quality control is data. In digitally mature environments, sensors, logs, and performance metrics provide a continuous stream of information about how products behave under real-world conditions. These data points offer more than fault detection, they reveal trends. A consistent deviation in temperature tolerance might indicate a design flaw. A slow degradation of part performance may suggest an upstream supplier quality issue. A jump in maintenance tickets from a specific region could signal inadequate onboarding or training. But none of these insights matter if no one is looking, or worse, if the data never reaches the product team.

Product managers must therefore advocate for closed-loop feedback systems. Quality data cannot live in isolation. If field teams detect defects, there must be a process to trace that defect back to the product design, supplier, or documentation. If customers report usability issues, those issues should trigger a product review, not just a service ticket. Quality becomes intelligent when it stops being reactive and starts shaping decisions. And that shift only happens when product leaders invite quality into the heart of the roadmap, not as a blocker, but as a guide.

It's also important to recognize that quality is not just about defects, it's about expectation. A product can function without error and still fail to deliver value if it doesn't meet performance standards, doesn't integrate smoothly, or requires more support than anticipated. Intelligent quality control, therefore, includes serviceability, install complexity, and user satisfaction as part of its scope. This is especially critical in systems where the product is not a standalone item, but a component in a larger operational ecosystem. If the product slows down the system, it's not high quality. If it forces unnecessary workarounds, it's not high quality. And if it frustrates the people who have to maintain it, it's not high quality, no matter what the inspection report says.

In highly regulated industries, quality also intersects with compliance. Standards are not suggestions; they are baselines. Meeting them is the minimum. Product managers must understand the certifications, audits, and documentation requirements tied to their products, especially when those products are involved in pressure systems, hazardous environments, or mission-critical operations. Compliance isn't just about passing a test, it's about being inspection-ready at all times. That means your documentation must reflect the real product. Your processes must match your declarations. Your people must be trained, and your controls must be active, not just performative.

Where intelligent quality systems truly shine is when they move from control to improvement. A traditional quality mindset asks: "Did this meet the standard?" A modern one asks: "How could this have been better?" Quality, when viewed through the lens of learning, becomes a growth engine. Every failure becomes a data point. Every inspection becomes a mirror. Every complaint becomes a roadmap. This mindset doesn't make quality softer, it makes it sharper. Because it focuses not just on compliance, but on continuous advantage.

The role of the product manager is to hold that tension. To ensure that quality is not buried under pressure. To protect the customer's experience, the company's credibility, and the operator's trust. Intelligent quality control is not about catching fewer mistakes, it's about making better choices earlier. And in the systems that drive our energy infrastructure, that kind of intelligence isn't optional, it's foundational.

One of the most underestimated aspects of quality assurance in energy and manufacturing environments is its emotional weight. When quality fails, the burden doesn't just land on the product, it lands on the people. Operators are the ones who deal with system malfunctions in the middle of the night. Engineers are the ones who face management when delivery timelines are missed. Technicians are the ones blamed when safety checks are failed or when a product behaves unpredictably. When quality breaks down, it creates not only operational tension but human strain; fatigue, distrust, rework cycles, and blame games that can corrode team morale and erode credibility faster than any spreadsheet ever shows.

This is why intelligent quality models cannot be reduced to defect tracking. They must acknowledge how problems are experienced in the field, and how those experiences can either inform future improvements or quietly disappear into institutional silence. The most advanced product systems fail when the culture discourages speaking up about recurring issues. And the most basic systems can thrive when quality reporting is seen not as an act of criticism, but as an act of contribution. That culture starts with how product managers respond. Do they investigate? Do they close the loop? Do they use quality data as a feedback system, or as a punishment mechanism?

What further complicates quality control in large-scale product environments is the distributed nature of responsibility. A product may be designed in one location, sourced in another, assembled in a third, and installed in a fourth. At each stage, someone assumes the previous party handled quality. And by the time a problem surfaces, no one is sure who owns it. This diffusion of accountability is where intelligent quality models provide real leverage, by making quality traceable, not just observable. The product manager's job, in this case, is to create clear checkpoints and reference systems so that quality becomes a trail, not a blame game.

This trail is especially important when it comes to vendor and supplier integration. In modern supply chains, very few products are made entirely in-house. External vendors provide components, services, subassemblies, and tooling. Each one of those parts has its own quality standards, tolerances, and failure points. The risk here is not just variability, it's invisibility. If a supplier downgrades a material, changes a process, or experiences labor turnover that affects consistency, the impact may not surface until much later; on the product, in the hands of the end user. Intelligent quality control requires proactive supplier engagement, not just through audits, but through ongoing relationship management.

This means asking more than "Did it pass inspection?" It means asking "Has anything changed since last quarter?" "What's trending differently in your internal QA?" "Can we align our definitions of acceptable variance?" The goal isn't to police vendors, it's to bring them into the lifecycle conversation. If they understand the product's end-use context, they're more likely to flag decisions that might compromise performance. If they feel accountable, they're more likely to share risks before those risks escalate. But if quality is outsourced without context, failure becomes a matter of time, not probability.

Documentation plays a role here too, especially in high-regulation industries. Every quality event should create a record, not just for compliance, but for pattern recognition. A single event may be a fluke. Three events may signal a systemic problem. But without the discipline of logging, categorizing, and reviewing quality issues across time and geography, the insights disappear. Worse, the same mistakes repeat across sites, products, or teams without anyone realizing it's déjà vu.

In intelligent quality models, these records become the backbone of continuous improvement. Every product issue becomes a line of inquiry. Every fix becomes a future-proofing opportunity. And every success becomes a baseline to protect. This shift; from defensive quality to offensive quality, is how product teams begin to lead, not just monitor. They stop waiting for failure to signal action. They start using evidence to shape better upstream design decisions, tighter downstream integration, and a culture where quality is expected, not exceptional.

Because in the supply chain world, quality is never just about what the product is—it's about what the product enables. A reliable part enables uptime. A smooth installation enables speed. A clear label enables confidence. A system that works as promised enables trust. And trust, more than anything, is what keeps teams aligned, customers loyal, and operations resilient.

That's what intelligent quality is really about. It's not perfection. It's not rigidity. It's not inspection for inspection's sake. It's about building products that can withstand time, change, pressure, and people, and still do what they were made to do.

5.1 Designing Quality Into the Process, Not Testing It at the End

One of the most persistent myths in product management, especially in supply chain-driven sectors like energy, is that quality is something you verify after the product is complete. That if it passes inspection, it's good. That if no red flags show up during delivery, the product is safe. But real quality; durable, systemic, operationally efficient quality, isn't the result of final checks. It's the result of what's embedded in the process from the very beginning.

Products that are designed with quality as an afterthought are more expensive to fix, harder to scale, and more likely to fail in the field. Every time a product fails an inspection, or triggers a warranty claim, or needs to be recalled, it's not just a defect being flagged, it's a late-stage cost being paid for an early-stage oversight. And this is where product managers can play an outsized role: by ensuring that the decisions made in concept, design, procurement, and scheduling all reflect the standards of performance that will eventually be demanded downstream.

Designing for quality starts with context. What conditions will this product face? What is its failure tolerance? Who will install it, operate it, maintain it? What tools will they have? What pressures will they be under? These questions help teams move from abstract quality definitions; checklists and specs—to actionable requirements that reflect real-world usage. A sensor, for instance, that meets temperature specifications in lab conditions may still fail when mounted in a space with heavy vibration and fluctuating humidity. But if no one asks how it's being mounted, or how often it will be cleaned, the issue won't emerge until failure hits.

When product managers push quality upstream, they stop relying solely on QA teams to catch what design didn't prevent. They start creating workflows where fewer things can go wrong in the first place. That means engaging suppliers early to agree on critical tolerances. It means involving the QA lead during prototyping, not just during handoff. It means ensuring that operators review installation steps, not just engineers. And it means incorporating field feedback into product iteration cycles long before issues become recurring complaints.

Process-integrated quality also changes how organizations measure success. Instead of tracking how many defects are caught, teams begin tracking how few are created. Instead of celebrating fast shipping, they ask how much rework followed. Instead of treating quality control as a safety net, they treat it as a reflection of design clarity and system fluency. And over time, this upstream mindset builds something bigger than compliance, it builds confidence.

In complex supply chains, where one weak link can affect an entire operation, quality must be systemic. It cannot depend on heroic effort at the last mile. It must be designed in, through specification, standardization, collaboration, and foresight. Because in product management, the best inspection is the one that confirms what everyone already knew: that the product was built right, not just built fast.

5.2 Creating Feedback Loops Between Field Performance and Product Design

One of the biggest breakdowns in quality management doesn't happen during manufacturing, it happens after deployment. A product enters the field, gets used in real-world conditions, and starts revealing truths that no simulation or inspection line ever captured. And yet, in many organizations, this field performance data never makes it back to the product team in time, or in a form that can be acted upon. The loop stays open. Issues get patched. Complaints get handled. But the root cause remains untouched, buried under operational urgency and disconnected systems.

This is where intelligent quality control becomes more than defect tracking, it becomes a strategy for continuous refinement. By building structured feedback loops between the people using the product and the people improving it, quality moves from being reactive to regenerative. The product gets smarter not just through testing, but through exposure. And the organization learns, not just from failure, but from context.

The field is full of signals: support tickets that hint at usability gaps, maintenance logs that reflect misalignment or wear, return reasons that suggest design oversights, workarounds that point to friction in the system. But these signals are often fragmented. They live in separate tools, different departments, or informal conversations that never leave the site. Intelligent quality systems recognize these data points as gold, and create channels to capture, analyze, and redistribute them where they matter most.

For product managers, this means treating the field not as the final stop, but as a learning lab. It means reviewing not just what failed, but what almost failed. It means asking operators what they changed and why. It means building mechanisms; surveys, digital forms, automated alerts, field interviews, periodic reviews, that invite field teams to contribute to product evolution. And more importantly, it means acting on what they share.

Creating these feedback loops also improves morale. When operators see that their frustrations lead to product improvements, their engagement shifts. When maintenance teams are asked for insight, not just compliance, they contribute more openly. And when the product team incorporates those insights visibly into future iterations, trust builds. The quality system becomes participatory, not punitive.

In large organizations, these loops must be formalized. They cannot depend solely on personality or individual initiative. That might mean a shared issue-tracking platform with direct line-of-sight for product and field teams. It might mean a quarterly field performance review with structured product takeaways. It might mean including service and support roles in product planning cycles. Whatever the format, the goal is the same: to shrink the distance between what happens in the field and what gets built into the next version.

Because real-world performance is the only test that counts. And the product that evolves fastest from it, not the one that tests cleanest in the lab, is the one that wins in the long run.

5.3 Using Quality as a Competitive Advantage, Not Just a Compliance Obligation

For many product teams, especially in regulated industries like energy and manufacturing, quality is treated as a minimum bar to clear. The thinking is simple: pass the audits, meet the specs, avoid fines. But this mindset reduces quality to paperwork; when in reality, it can be a sharp competitive edge. In today's industrial ecosystem, where downtime is costly and client expectations are high, consistent quality becomes more than an internal KPI. It becomes a market differentiator. A brand promise. A reason customers stay loyal.

Quality as compliance is passive. It says, "We did what was required." But quality as a competitive advantage is active. It says, "We built this to perform, to last, and to make your work easier." This shift in posture, from obligation to intention; changes how a product is designed, communicated, and supported. And it gives product managers new tools to compete, even in markets where features or pricing may be similar across vendors.

Consider two vendors offering similar industrial components. One promises faster delivery. The other promises a defect rate below 0.5% over five years, proven, audited, and backed by transparent logs. The second vendor may be slightly more expensive, but the message is clear: you'll spend less on troubleshooting, less on downtime, less on customer escalation. And for enterprise clients or operators who have seen what happens when quality fails, that peace of mind is often worth more than a discount.

Intelligent product teams build toward this trust deliberately. They don't just state quality claims, they demonstrate them. They publish inspection reports, reliability metrics, long-term field performance summaries. They work with marketing to translate technical reliability into customer reassurance. They turn ISO certifications or performance guarantees into actual selling points, not footnotes. And in doing so, they shift the conversation: from "Is this product good enough?" to "Is this product the safer bet?"

Even in internal product settings, where the customer is another division or region; quality can be a leverage point. A team that delivers stable, clean, well-documented systems becomes a preferred partner. Their products get integrated faster, receive less resistance, and stay in use longer. Why? Because people trust the quality. And trust, once earned, lowers friction in every subsequent interaction.

Product managers who see this clearly stop treating quality as a task for someone else. They begin investing in it strategically. They anticipate where customers might lose confidence and shore up those weaknesses. They clarify tolerances, document performance boundaries, and make bold claims only when they're sure those claims can withstand real-world pressure. This is not perfectionism. It's performance-driven leadership.

And in energy and manufacturing, where decisions are high-stakes, rollout cycles are long, and operational reliability is everything, this kind of leadership is rare. Which is exactly why it stands out.

5.4 Building a Culture of Quality Ownership Across Functions

No system, however well-designed, can sustain quality without people who take ownership. And yet, in many energy and supply chain operations, quality is still seen as someone else's job. Engineers build. Procurement sources. Technicians install. Inspectors inspect. But when something breaks, no one wants to hold the mirror. This fragmented sense of accountability is one of the greatest threats to sustainable product performance. And it's precisely where culture comes in, not the vague, motivational kind, but the practical kind that defines how work gets done and who takes responsibility when things go sideways.

Building a culture of quality ownership doesn't mean turning everyone into QA specialists. It means creating an environment where quality is seen as everyone's job—because everyone touches it. It starts with language. When leaders talk about quality as a value, not just a metric, it signals to teams that quality is not just an end-of-line concern. It matters in the specs you write, the parts you source, the shortcuts you don't take, the corners you choose not to cut. When these ideas show up in onboarding, team rituals, performance reviews, and project planning, they stick.

But culture doesn't change through words alone, it changes through systems. People take ownership of what they can influence. That means giving teams visibility into quality performance, not just across products, but within their part of the process. A technician should be able to see how install errors trend over time. A buyer should be able to view vendor quality scores. A designer should be shown where a tolerance choice affected downstream serviceability. When that transparency exists, people start adjusting their decisions before they're asked to.

Ownership also grows when teams are trusted to flag risks without fear. In many industrial settings, quality issues are buried, not because people don't care, but because they're tired of being blamed. This leads to a toxic loop: silence, failure, then reactive escalation. But when quality problems are treated as system signals, not individual indictments, people begin to speak up earlier. They offer suggestions. They bring concerns. They raise their hand when something feels off. This isn't about eliminating mistakes. It's about giving those mistakes somewhere to land and something to teach.

The product manager plays a unique role here. As the connector between functions, they can reinforce a standard of shared responsibility. They can ask hard questions across teams: "Did we test this under real operating conditions?" "Has operations signed off on the maintenance procedure?" "Has this vendor met their last three cycle targets?" These aren't confrontational questions; they're alignment questions. And when asked consistently, they help teams think cross-functionally. They prevent finger-pointing by creating visibility before failure. And they remind everyone that quality isn't a phase, it's a posture.

Ultimately, a culture of quality doesn't make mistakes disappear. But it makes them easier to see, easier to share, and easier to fix. It creates a climate where excellence isn't just demanded from a department, it's expected from the system. And in product environments where reliability is currency, that expectation becomes the true engine of long-term success.

CHAPTER 6

Risk Management and Safety in Product Strategy

In product management, risk is not just a possibility, it's a constant. Especially in the energy and manufacturing sectors, where products don't exist in isolation but interact with complex machinery, volatile environments, and strict regulations, risk is everywhere. A miscalculation in temperature thresholds. A sourcing decision that introduces variability. A miscommunication that results in the wrong installation procedure. These aren't edge cases, they're everyday exposures. And the product manager's job isn't to eliminate risk entirely; it's to understand it, surface it, and manage it with discipline.

For too long, risk has been framed as a reactive discipline. Something reviewed when things go wrong. Something relegated to safety managers or legal teams. But modern product management recognizes that risk strategy is product strategy.

Every product decision, what to build, how to build it, where to deploy it, how to support it, carries trade-offs. And if those trade-offs aren't named, tracked, and calibrated, they show up later as cost, failure, liability, or delay.

Risk management in product work begins at the design phase. What assumptions are we making about the environment where this product will operate? What will happen if those assumptions break? What is the cost of a failure in this context, not just financially, but reputationally or physically? These questions don't slow the process down, they anchor it in reality. When product teams avoid these questions, they ship brittle systems that collapse under stress. But when they lean in, they create more resilient designs, more honest roadmaps, and more prepared support structures.

Risk isn't abstract. It shows up in specific decisions. A pressure gauge sourced from a lower-cost supplier may meet technical specifications, but what's the risk if that supplier has weaker quality assurance processes? A software update may streamline controls, but what's the risk if field operators are not retrained before rollout? A hardware redesign may improve modularity, but what's the risk of integration failure with existing legacy systems on-site? Each of these risks is a design variable, and intelligent product managers treat them as such.

Where risk and safety intersect most visibly is in field operations. A product that fails in a lab may waste time. A product that fails in a pressurized environment, near live systems or critical infrastructure, can cause injury or worse. This is why safety cannot be retrofitted. It must be built into every layer, from material selection to installation guidelines to maintenance routines. Product managers must work closely with HSE (Health, Safety, and Environment) teams, compliance officers, and operational leads to ensure that every product released into the field meets not only internal performance goals but external risk thresholds that protect people and systems alike.

This means understanding the difference between **inherent risk** and **residual risk**. Inherent risk is what the system carries naturally; high voltage, heat, pressure, weight. Residual risk is what remains after controls, mitigations, and design choices are applied. The product manager's job is to shrink residual risk without creating operational drag. This may involve adding sensor redundancy, providing clear fail-safes, limiting exposure time during installation, or designing systems that fail safely under stress.

Product managers must also manage perceived risk, the gap between what a system is designed to handle and what the user believes it can handle. If operators mistrust a component, even if it's technically sound; they may bypass it, misuse it, or ignore alerts. If support teams don't fully understand a new system's behavior, they may escalate unnecessarily or respond too late. This is why clear communication, training, and transparency are all part of risk management. A safe product is not just one that works well, it's one that is understood well.

Another layer is operational risk, the things that go wrong not because the product is faulty, but because the environment is unpredictable. Storms. Labor shortages. Supply bottlenecks. Human fatigue. Regulatory changes. The product team doesn't control these variables, but it must design with them in mind. That means building buffers into timelines, alternate configurations for installation, flexibility in component sourcing, and clarity around support escalation pathways. It means acknowledging that things will go wrong, and designing for recovery, not just success.

In energy and manufacturing, the most respected product teams are not the ones that avoid all risks. They are the ones that know which risks they're carrying, and have built systems strong enough to withstand them. They communicate openly, plan conservatively, act decisively, and never treat safety as an inconvenience. They understand that risk is not the opposite of innovation, it is the cost of doing meaningful work in real-world systems.

A risk-aware product team doesn't slow down progress. It enables sustainable progress. It prevents small issues from snowballing. It protects the company's credibility. It makes bold moves with clear eyes. And over time, it becomes the team that others look to when the stakes are high and failure is not an option.

Because in product management, especially in sectors where reliability and safety define survival, risk isn't something to be avoided. It's something to be led.

6.1 Embedding Risk Assessment into Day-to-Day Decision Making

In many organizations, risk is something you document once; during kickoff meetings, funding reviews, or compliance checklists, and then set aside. It becomes a box to tick, a folder on the server, a reference point only when things start going wrong. But this approach isolates risk from where it actually lives: in the everyday decisions that shape a product's performance, reliability, and exposure. Real risk management isn't episodic, it's embedded. It lives in the hundreds of small choices that happen long before launch, and long after delivery.

To embed risk into everyday product work, teams need more than policies, they need patterns. Teams must be trained to ask the right questions at the right moments: What are the worst-case scenarios for this decision? What systems would break if this assumption is wrong? What are we accepting by default, simply because it's "how it's always been done"? This kind of thinking isn't fear-based, it's foresight-based. And when it becomes part of the rhythm of decision-making, it prevents the kind of systemic risk that tends to hide in operational blind spots.

For example, when selecting between two vendors, a traditional product decision might prioritize cost, lead time, or existing relationships. But with embedded risk thinking, the conversation shifts. What's this vendor's history of compliance with safety-critical components? How easily can their manufacturing be audited? What happens to our delivery timeline if their region is disrupted by logistics or regulation? These are not niche concerns, they're survival-level considerations, especially in high-stakes industries like oil & gas, heavy manufacturing, or power infrastructure.

Embedding risk into the product development flow also means identifying key decision thresholds; moments where risk exposure either narrows or expands dramatically. This might include decisions like introducing a new material into a pressure-sensitive system, changing firmware on a field-deployed device, switching from human inspection to automated quality checks, or altering field install procedures without full retraining. At each of these points, product managers must slow down enough to ask not "Can we?" but "Should we, and what if we're wrong?"

To support this, product teams should maintain living risk registers, not buried in spreadsheets, but integrated into product management tools, sprint reviews, and roadmap planning. These registers aren't just for high-profile risks. They should include low-probability, high-impact scenarios, unclear ownership zones, or evolving assumptions that need rechecking. The goal is not to build a perfect list, it's to normalize risk visibility and decision hygiene.

Another practice that strengthens embedded risk management is the use of pre-mortems, structured exercises where teams imagine future failure and reverse-engineer the likely causes. This pushes teams to acknowledge what they've overlooked, what they've assumed, or where they're rushing. It's not a prediction exercise, it's an insight generator. And the risks surfaced here often become early triggers for mitigation long before the issues escalate.

Ultimately, embedding risk into daily decisions changes the product culture. It encourages humility without hesitation. It turns speculation into scenario planning. And it equips teams to move with speed and confidence, not because they've eliminated uncertainty, but because they've mapped its terrain.

In the environments where product decisions carry real weight; on safety, revenue, uptime, or environmental impact, this kind of embedded thinking doesn't slow teams down. It makes them sharper. Smarter. And far less likely to be surprised when pressure hits.

6.2 Cross-Functional Alignment as a Risk Mitigation Tool

When risk shows up in product systems, it rarely appears in one place. The problem may be a design flaw, but the consequence hits in operations. The root cause might stem from procurement, but it lands as a missed customer SLA. Or a minor issue flagged in QA may snowball into a reputational crisis when support teams aren't prepared. This fragmentation of risk is exactly why product managers must lead not just from the roadmap, but from the seams; those cross-functional boundaries where accountability is often blurry, but impact is most profound.

Cross-functional collaboration isn't just a matter of working together, it's a critical layer of risk mitigation. Every team sees risk differently. Legal sees liability. Operations sees downtime. Finance sees exposure. Field teams see danger. If these perspectives aren't intentionally brought together, products are developed in silos and blind spots multiply. But when risk is approached collectively, patterns emerge early. Assumptions are challenged before they harden into failures. And dependencies are clarified before they become friction points under stress.

This is why some of the most effective risk reviews don't happen in boardrooms, they happen in alignment meetings between engineering, field ops, QA, compliance, and procurement. They happen in pre-launch simulations where every function is asked, "What's most likely to go wrong, and how do we prevent it?" They happen when feedback from each department is not just requested, but acted upon. In these environments, risk management becomes a shared language, not a departmental turf.

To make this sustainable, product teams must create routines for cross-functional insight, not just ad hoc escalations. That might look like:

- Cross-functional sign-offs at key lifecycle milestones
- Real-time issue tracking dashboards shared across functions
- Risk walkthroughs that involve stakeholders from legal, HSE, and service teams
- Regular syncs that ask, "What are you worried about that we might be missing?"

This approach doesn't eliminate surprises. But it makes teams better equipped to respond without scrambling, because the relational capital is already in place, and the conversation around risk has already been normalized.

In complex systems, no one team owns the whole picture. But when cross-functional collaboration becomes a habit, not just an event; organizations start making decisions with sharper eyes and steadier hands.

6.3 Planning for Failure: Designing Systems That Recover with Control

In supply chain operations; especially in energy, heavy manufacturing, and infrastructure, failure is not a theoretical risk. It's a given. No matter how well a system is designed, eventually, something breaks. A machine overheats. A shipment gets delayed. A component wears out early. A user misinterprets an alert. The difference between a crisis and a contained incident isn't whether failure happens, it's how prepared the system is to absorb it.

Yet, many product teams still design for the ideal. The workflow that assumes every input is valid. The component that assumes perfect handling. The software that assumes stable connectivity. These assumptions don't hold in the field. And when the system can't flex, it snaps.

This is where graceful failure becomes a product design discipline. It's not just about redundancy or backups. It's about resilience, building systems that know how to pause, notify, reroute, and recover without spiraling. A failed component that isolates safely, rather than causing a cascade. A digital interface that provides fallback instructions when connectivity drops. A mechanical design that prevents incorrect assembly. These are not glamorous features, but they are the features that protect performance when stress hits.

Product managers must ask: What happens when this fails? Who will notice first? What will they do next? And will they have what they need to respond without confusion or panic? Answering these questions leads to clearer documentation, more thoughtful user prompts, better escalation protocols, and smarter interface design.

Failure planning also involves post-incident learning. Every disruption, no matter how small, contains a lesson. But most organizations don't have the feedback systems in place to extract it. Once the issue is resolved, the focus returns to delivery. The insight is lost. But when teams hold structured postmortems; not to assign blame, but to deepen understanding, they create a culture where failure becomes a lever for system strength.

Ultimately, designing for failure is not pessimism. It's maturity. It recognizes that what makes a product trustworthy is not that it never fails, but that when it does, it fails softly, predictably, and recoverably. In sectors where lives, assets, and reputations are on the line, that kind of reliability isn't a luxury. It's a standard.

CHAPTER 7

Strategic Procurement and Supplier Management in Product Delivery

Behind every high-performing product is a complex network of suppliers, vendors, and procurement decisions that shape what gets delivered, how reliably, and at what cost. For product managers, especially those operating within supply chain-intensive sectors like energy and manufacturing, procurement is not an afterthought, it's infrastructure. A product's strength, speed to market, and longevity often depend less on what happens at the whiteboard and more on what happens in contracts, lead times, and supplier relationships.

Too often, procurement is treated as a separate function; looped in after specifications are finalized and timelines are set. But in reality, procurement decisions carry enormous influence over design constraints, production timelines, quality thresholds, and scalability. If a supplier can't meet compliance requirements, the product can't ship. If a component has a 16-week lead time and no substitutes, the launch stalls. If a vendor switches materials without flagging it, performance degrades silently until a field failure prompts escalation. These risks aren't operational, they're strategic. And managing them requires the product manager to be actively involved in procurement conversations, not just reacting to them.

Strategic procurement starts with clarity. What are the critical components of this product; parts without which function, safety, or performance will suffer? Which vendors supply them? What is our exposure if any one of those vendors defaults, changes terms, or experiences geopolitical disruption? Strategic product managers map this out early, identifying **single points of failure** and building alternatives before they're needed. This could mean dual-sourcing critical parts, pre-qualifying backup vendors, or designing components with modularity in mind to allow sourcing flexibility without redesign.

Beyond the hardware or materials, supplier relationships also define product reliability. A vendor who meets specs but ignores change management processes can derail a product's lifecycle without ever breaking a rule. A vendor who's technically sound but fails to communicate shifts in process, personnel, or upstream supply introduces instability into the product environment. This is why supplier management isn't just a purchasing function, it's a visibility function. Product managers must work with procurement to create feedback-rich relationships with suppliers, where transparency and proactive reporting are built into the rhythm of collaboration.

In mature systems, this often includes:

- Regular performance reviews with key vendors
- Shared forecasts and planning horizons
- Joint quality investigations when issues arise
- Alignment on sustainability, ethics, and compliance expectations
- Early supplier involvement in product redesign and testing

These practices turn vendors into partners. And when the supplier becomes a stakeholder in the product's success, not just its shipment, the entire ecosystem becomes stronger.

Pricing is another layer of complexity. In fast-moving markets, cost pressure is real. But cutting procurement cost at the expense of lifecycle cost is a mistake too many teams repeat. The cheapest component may require more frequent replacement. The most accessible vendor may have weaker QA. The fastest lead time may come from suppliers with low traceability. Strategic procurement doesn't mean chasing the lowest number, it means negotiating the best value over time. And for product managers, this means being able to articulate what that value looks like: fewer defects, smoother integration, better compliance alignment, or lower cost of failure in the field.

One of the most powerful things a product team can do is establish procurement-readiness criteria during the product planning phase. These are guardrails that prevent last-minute changes from introducing risk: a minimum set of supplier certifications, a material traceability requirement, a performance record threshold, or alignment with ethical sourcing guidelines. When these standards are defined and enforced, the procurement team can act with speed and confidence, knowing that every selected vendor already supports the product's strategic intent.

Supplier management also extends into lifecycle support. Once the product is launched, vendors still matter. They supply spares. Support warranty repairs. Contribute to redesigns. Respond to field failures. Product teams that abandon the supplier relationship after launch often find themselves scrambling when a small issue needs a fast resolution. But when relationships are maintained, through structured contact, mutual accountability, and real data sharing; vendors respond faster, troubleshoot better, and stand behind the product when it counts.

And finally, supplier diversity, resilience, and geography are no longer back-office considerations, they are frontline strategy. The past decade has shown just how fragile global supply chains can be. Political tension, climate disruption, labor shortages, and compliance crackdowns can destabilize even the most predictable partners. Product managers who understand this reality don't panic when it hits. They've already mapped alternatives, flagged exposures, and collaborated with procurement on strategies for continuity.

In energy, manufacturing, and infrastructure, a product is only as stable as the supply chain that sustains it. And a product manager is only as prepared as the procurement system that supports them. This is why supplier strategy is product strategy. It determines not just what can be built, but whether it will be delivered, adopted, and sustained under pressure.

The best product managers treat procurement not as a transaction, but as a collaboration. And over time, those relationships become a quiet source of excellence, protecting performance when the market shifts, pressure rises, and every decision matters more than usual.

These moments don't always make the headlines, but they can derail months of work and force last-minute design changes, procurement scrambles, and field-level workarounds that stretch already-thin teams. In supply chain-heavy industries, this kind of risk is not rare. It's baked into the complexity of global sourcing. And product managers who treat it as someone else's problem often find themselves firefighting with limited options.

This is why vendor risk mapping must be part of early product planning, not just left to procurement dashboards. It's not enough to know whether a supplier can meet today's demand. The question is: how exposed are we if that supplier drops off the map tomorrow? What components are at highest risk of interruption? Which ones are region-locked? Which vendors are operating at maximum capacity, and which ones have room to grow with us? These aren't procurement-only insights. They're product dependencies. And smart product leaders are proactive in surfacing them.

Another gap that undermines product delivery is poor supplier onboarding. Even technically capable vendors can become liabilities if expectations are misaligned, documentation is unclear, or change management protocols aren't enforced. This often happens when sourcing happens under time pressure; vendors are approved quickly, specs are shared loosely, and the assumption is that everything will "settle in" during production. But in reality, that early sloppiness sets the stage for preventable mistakes. Tolerances get misread. Compliance gets delayed. Response times lag. And the product team ends up absorbing the impact of incomplete alignment.

Strategic product managers push for thorough onboarding, regardless of vendor reputation or past performance. This includes sharing not just part specs, but full context: operating conditions, user behavior, downstream integration points, and anticipated lifecycle performance. It includes defining escalation paths, response time expectations, communication protocols, and approval flows for process changes. These aren't bureaucratic steps, they're risk controls. And when they're skipped, the product carries hidden liabilities that only surface when it's too late.

As product complexity grows, the number of suppliers involved often increases. With that comes inter-supplier risk, where one vendor's delay or quality issue affects another's output, and no one claims responsibility. This kind of systemic risk is particularly dangerous because it tends to slip through cracks in ownership. But a product manager with visibility into the full supplier web can begin to trace these dependencies and design buffers or sequencing that reduce exposure. For example, if two components require final integration on-site, but one has historically inconsistent delivery, that risk can be mitigated by adjusting production schedules, increasing local stock, or pre-building partial assemblies.

One area where supplier alignment is especially crucial is in product iteration cycles. As products evolve, through redesigns, updates, or feedback-driven improvements; suppliers must adapt in lockstep. If vendors are not kept in the loop or given adequate time to adjust, the result is either misaligned parts or rushed changes that compromise quality. A high-performing product ecosystem ensures that every change in the roadmap is communicated clearly, with enough context for suppliers to assess feasibility, impact, and timeline before production begins. That level of coordination isn't easy, but it's what separates reactive supply chains from agile, responsive ones.

Technology can help. Shared digital portals, collaborative supplier platforms, integrated quality and documentation systems, all of these tools help create **shared truth** between product and procurement teams. But technology alone is not enough. What matters is the culture behind it. Do suppliers feel like partners or interchangeable vendors? Are they incentivized to flag concerns early, or do they fear being replaced? Is procurement operating as a cost enforcer or as a value architect alongside the product team?

When the culture is right, and the relationships are built on mutual visibility and shared accountability, supplier partnerships become a strategic asset. They enable agility when demand surges, they provide insight when design evolves, and they help shield the product from external shocks, whether they come from politics, raw material shortages, or shifts in customer expectations.

7.1 Early Supplier Involvement (ESI): Designing with Your Vendors, Not After Them

One of the most quietly damaging habits in product organizations is treating suppliers as late-stage executors, looped in after the designs are finalized, the specs are locked, and the timeline is already ticking. In this model, suppliers are simply asked to deliver, regardless of whether the product design makes sense for manufacturability, logistics, or sustained quality. This approach creates tension, invites misalignment, and often leads to downstream issues that are expensive to fix and frustrating to navigate.

Early Supplier Involvement (ESI) flips that model. It brings suppliers into the product development process during the early design stages; when ideas are still taking shape, and decisions are still reversible. The logic is simple: your suppliers know things you don't. They understand material behavior under stress, the hidden cost drivers of certain finishes, the tolerance windows that can make or break automation compatibility, the best packaging configurations for shipment efficiency, and even regulatory nuances across different regions. Ignoring that knowledge is a liability. Harnessing it is a competitive advantage.

When suppliers are engaged early, they contribute design feedback that prevents rework. They flag feasibility issues before prototypes are built. They propose lower-cost alternatives that don't compromise performance. They suggest modular approaches that simplify inventory management or improve assembly speed. They highlight long lead items that could delay delivery if not accounted for in time. And they offer insights that make the final product stronger, more scalable, and easier to support in the field.

But ESI doesn't just benefit the product, it improves the relationship. Suppliers who are invited in early feel respected. They develop a stake in the product's success. They collaborate more openly, escalate issues faster, and commit resources more willingly. The dynamic shifts from "us vs. them" to "we're building this together." And in moments of stress, when a deadline slips, a spec changes, or a crisis emerges, that trust becomes the cushion that keeps everything from falling apart.

To make ESI work, structure is key. It's not about looping every supplier into every meeting, it's about identifying critical suppliers whose input can shape product outcomes and building intentional moments for them to engage. This might include:

- Early design reviews with supplier engineering teams
- Pre-prototype material sourcing consultations
- Co-developed test plans for performance validation
- Joint workshops to explore manufacturability constraints
- Regular updates during the design refinement phase

For the product manager, this means opening the design process without losing ownership. It means balancing internal priorities with external wisdom. And it means creating a space where suppliers can speak candidly, not just about what they can deliver, but about what the product could become.

Because in a supply chain-driven world, innovation doesn't just come from inside your building. Sometimes, the smartest design move is simply to ask the people who've built it a hundred times before, and give them room to help you build it better.

7.2 Building Multi-Tier Visibility Across the Supply Chain

One of the most dangerous assumptions in product delivery is that your supplier's reliability guarantees your own. In reality, risk often lives further down the chain, at the sub-supplier level, in tier 2 and tier 3 relationships that most product teams never see. A component may arrive on time, but the materials used in that component may be facing rising regulatory scrutiny. A part may pass quality inspection, but its internal electronics may be coming from a region with rising geopolitical tension. If your visibility ends at your direct supplier, your resilience is already compromised.

Multi-tier visibility is not just about transparency, it's about foresight. It's the ability to anticipate slow-moving disruptions before they explode into urgent problems. It's understanding not just who supplies your supplier, but what could affect their ability to keep supplying. And it's one of the clearest differentiators between reactive product organizations and strategically stable ones.

For product managers, gaining this visibility doesn't mean micromanaging the entire supplier ecosystem. It means collaborating with procurement and supply chain teams to identify critical dependencies, map tiered relationships for key components, and establish trigger points for deeper investigation. This isn't just a logistics exercise, it's a strategic one. Because when a shortage emerges, or a regulation changes, or a natural disaster hits a key production region, the teams that already know where their exposures are will respond faster; and with far less chaos.

Multi-tier visibility supports better design, too. If you know that a critical part relies on a single factory in a flood-prone region, you can push for alternative configurations. If a supplier's vendor sources rare earth minerals under increasing export restrictions, you can adjust specs to reduce vulnerability. These aren't just defensive moves, they're decisions that keep your product roadmap intact when the world gets messy.

Technology plays a role here; platforms that integrate supplier data, track sub-tier inputs, and flag anomalies across geographies and compliance frameworks. But technology is only as good as the culture it supports. Many suppliers still resist sharing sub-tier data, fearing exposure or competitive disadvantage. This is where relationship strength matters. Product managers can't force visibility, but they can earn it by building trust, framing requests in terms of shared risk, and making it clear that multi-tier insight helps everyone respond better under pressure.

In sectors where the supply chain is as complex as the product itself, visibility becomes currency. It allows teams to make better trade-offs, flag problems before they become crises, and lead conversations with vendors from a place of preparedness, not panic.

The lesson is simple: you can't control what you can't see. But when you start seeing further, you don't just manage risk, you reshape it.

7.3 Creating Supplier Ecosystems That Grow with the Product

Every successful product eventually faces a moment when its needs outgrow its original support structure. Volumes increase. Territories expand. New features require new parts. Regulatory expectations shift. What once worked smoothly with a handful of suppliers becomes fragile when scaled. And if the supplier ecosystem can't evolve with the product, what once felt like reliability begins to feel like friction.

This is why product managers must think beyond point-in-time sourcing. Instead of just asking, "Who can supply this now?" the better question is: "Which partners can grow with us?" Because what the product needs today; speed, flexibility, technical support, will evolve into something more complex: demand forecasting, custom engineering, regional fulfillment, and shared innovation. If the supplier isn't equipped, or willing, to grow alongside those demands, performance will eventually stall.

Building a scalable supplier ecosystem starts by identifying core vs. peripheral suppliers. Core suppliers are tied to your product's identity, either because they contribute to critical performance metrics or because their role is deeply integrated into your systems and processes. These are the partners worth investing in: onboarding them thoroughly, aligning on long-term roadmaps, and involving them in early-stage planning cycles. Peripheral suppliers, on the other hand, can be managed more flexibly, rotated as needed, or diversified for cost and logistics balance.

Scalable ecosystems also require technical range. Can your supplier support slight design changes without renegotiation? Can they prototype when needed? Do they have internal R&D capabilities or partnerships that allow them to support your product evolution, not just replicate what's been done? Suppliers that can only deliver what they already know become bottlenecks when innovation accelerates.

Another element is geographic agility. As product demand grows across regions, logistics costs, import regulations, and lead time variability become serious friction points. Suppliers who can support multi-regional fulfillment, local manufacturing, or cross-border compliance offer strategic leverage that enables smoother product expansion. That leverage isn't just operational, it's protective. It insulates the product from the shocks of local instability, currency fluctuation, and sudden policy changes.

Just as important is data maturity. Suppliers who track their own performance, integrate with your systems, and are capable of joint forecasting enable a level of collaboration that goes far beyond order fulfillment. With shared dashboards, automated restocking signals, and aligned inventory views, the product team can reduce uncertainty and respond to demand swings without constant firefighting. These aren't just efficiencies, they're safeguards against the chaos that breaks product trust at scale.

But perhaps the most underrated requirement for a scalable supplier ecosystem is cultural alignment. This includes shared values around quality, ethics, environmental impact, and partnership style. As scrutiny increases around how and where things are made, the character of your suppliers becomes part of your product's public narrative. A strong vendor today can become a reputational risk tomorrow if values drift, standards drop, or public perception shifts. Forward-thinking product managers assess this fit regularly, not just for compliance, but for alignment with where the company is headed and what it wants its products to represent.

CHAPTER 8

Sustainability and Circular Design in Supply Chain Product Strategy

In today's product landscape, sustainability is no longer a marketing angle or compliance checkbox, it's a strategic imperative. For supply chain-intensive sectors like energy, manufacturing, and infrastructure, the pressure to reduce waste, minimize environmental impact, and create regenerative systems is reshaping how products are designed, sourced, used, and retired. And while sustainability is often championed by ESG teams or regulatory mandates, the real work begins at the product level. That makes product managers key players in defining whether a company merely reduces harm, or creates value through circular, intelligent design.

At its core, sustainability in product management means designing with lifecycle awareness. It's asking: What happens to this product after it's delivered? How easy is it to maintain, repair, or upgrade? Can it be reused, recycled, or repurposed? What materials are being used, and how do they affect the planet, the people sourcing them, and the ability to re-enter the supply loop?

Circular design takes these questions further. Instead of viewing a product's end-of-life as disposal, it reimagines it as reintegration. A pump whose casing can be remanufactured. A device whose internal components are modular and swappable. A part designed with reclaimed alloys or biodegradable polymers. These are not science fiction ideas, they're the future of viable supply chains. And product managers are the ones with the proximity, planning authority, and system-level perspective to lead these shifts from vision to implementation.

But making sustainability real requires trade-offs. Recycled materials may have variable availability. Eco-designs may raise initial costs. Supplier vetting for ethical sourcing may slow down procurement. These pressures often clash with the day-to-day urgency of timelines, margins, and volume targets. And this is where leadership comes in. A product manager focused on sustainable strategy must be prepared to defend the long view: lower maintenance costs, stronger brand trust, reduced regulatory risk, and future readiness in a world moving aggressively toward environmental accountability.

One of the most practical ways product teams can embed sustainability is through material strategy. This starts by auditing what materials are being used, why they were chosen, and whether lower-impact alternatives exist. It includes identifying high-risk materials, those that are energy-intensive, non-renewable, toxic, or ethically problematic (such as conflict minerals or illegally logged timber). Once identified, those materials should be prioritized for redesign or substitution, with input from engineering, procurement, and suppliers who understand both performance implications and sourcing realities.

Another opportunity is in **design for disassembly**. Most products are optimized for cost-effective assembly, but fall apart unpredictably, expensively, or destructively. This makes repair hard, refurbishment unlikely, and recycling inefficient. But when a product is designed to come apart cleanly, through standardized fasteners, accessible components, and documented teardown sequences, it creates a second life. Modules can be upgraded without replacing the entire system. Materials can be sorted and recycled at higher rates. And support teams can respond faster, with less waste.

Sustainability also lives in logistics. Smart product managers partner with supply chain teams to reduce the environmental footprint of packaging, transportation, and warehousing. This can include consolidating shipments, minimizing air freight, optimizing container density, and using reusable packaging materials. It might seem minor, but multiplied across thousands of units and extended across global routes, the impact becomes massive. In many organizations, logistics accounts for more emissions than manufacturing. Product managers who engage early in these decisions can shift that reality without sacrificing performance.

Another area with massive upside is **lifecycle extension**. A product that performs reliably for 10 years generates less waste than one that needs replacement every 3. A device that can be updated via software or retrofitted for new functionality doesn't need to be discarded. And an asset that can be returned, reprocessed, and resold at end-of-life generates residual value while reducing landfill pressure. But this only works if durability is designed in, not bolted on. Materials must be selected for long-term resilience. Software must be built for updates. Documentation must support non-expert users. And business models must be structured to support reuse, refurbishment, or return incentives.

Of course, none of this happens in a vacuum. Regulatory pressure is increasing globally. From Europe's Right to Repair directives to extended producer responsibility (EPR) laws across Asia and Africa, governments are demanding that manufacturers take accountability for the full lifecycle of their products. Product managers who wait to be forced into compliance will pay a premium in the form of rushed redesigns, reputation damage, and rising fines. But those who anticipate these shifts, and lead from the front, can turn compliance into competitiveness.

Sustainability is not about perfection. It's about trajectory. Are we building products that degrade the system, or strengthen it? Are we ignoring waste, or designing around it? Are we treating resources as disposable, or as part of a closed, intelligent loop? These aren't just questions for executives. They are the product manager's questions. Because how a product is made, maintained, and retired is inseparable from how it is experienced. And in a world where ecological limits are hardening, the most valuable products will be those that respect them.

Leading sustainable product strategies isn't about saying the right thing. It's about doing the hard thing, making thoughtful trade-offs, challenging legacy assumptions, and showing that responsible design isn't a burden, it's a blueprint for resilience.

What they lack is agreement. Between departments. Between incentives. Between timelines. A sustainable option might exist, but if procurement is measured on cost savings alone, operations on delivery speed, and product teams on launch dates, the system rejects anything that slows the cycle down, even if it leads to long-term value.

This is why sustainability must be treated as a cross-functional commitment, not a department's responsibility. Product managers are uniquely positioned to be the connective tissue in this effort. They can frame sustainable design not as a constraint, but as a shared goal that makes everyone's outcomes better. They can host trade-off conversations early, before decisions get locked in. They can bring procurement into material selection, loop operations into packaging redesigns, and invite marketing into the conversation about telling a more honest story.

But none of this works without visibility. To drive circular product strategy, product teams need to understand the environmental cost of their current designs. That means working with sustainability officers, ESG analysts, or data teams to capture real metrics, embodied carbon, water usage, landfill impact, or ethical sourcing scores. These numbers don't need to be perfect, but they must be directional. Because what gets measured gets improved. And without a baseline, teams are flying blind.

Another critical layer is supplier accountability. Even if a company commits to greener products, it cannot meet its goals unless its supply chain is aligned. A product may be designed for recyclability, but if the vendor changes materials without flagging it, the loop breaks. A sustainability commitment may include labor ethics, but if sub-tier suppliers rely on underpaid or unsafe labor practices, reputational risk escalates quickly. Product managers must therefore play a more active role in supplier evaluation, not just for capability, but for alignment with sustainability and compliance expectations.

That means asking deeper questions: Where are your raw materials sourced? Are your facilities powered by renewable energy? What are your emissions targets, and how do they affect lead times? Have you passed environmental audits, and are your records transparent? These conversations may feel new, but they are rapidly becoming standard. And suppliers that resist transparency will eventually be replaced, not just for ethical reasons, but because their lack of visibility introduces unacceptable risk.

This is where systems thinking becomes critical. Sustainability cannot be tacked on after a product is developed. It must be woven into the ecosystem. The packaging decision affects return logistics. The modular design affects customer support protocols. The sourcing decision affects PR and compliance. Every part of the product affects something else. The job of the product manager is to hold this full view, and ensure the product is not just viable in the market, but responsible within its system.

One of the most exciting frontiers here is the use of digital product passports, centralized, shareable data sets that carry information about a product's material makeup, repair history, sourcing credentials, and recyclability. These passports make it easier for recyclers, field techs, and customers to interact responsibly with products. They also give companies traceability; helping them prove compliance, defend claims, and adjust to emerging regulations around material transparency and end-of-life accountability. Over time, these systems become the foundation for a regenerative product loop, where data isn't just captured, but reinvested into smarter design choices.

And that's the real promise of circular design. Not just that products become "less bad", but that they become better over time. As data flows back, as systems stabilize, and as incentives align, organizations start building differently. Not just because it's mandated, but because it's better for business. Retained value. Lower cost of support. Higher customer trust. Stronger compliance posture. And, in the truest sense of the word, long-term relevance.

In the past, the product manager's job was to build something that worked. Today, it's to build something that works, and keeps working, across ecosystems, lifecycles, and generations of use. That's not idealism. It's strategy. And the product teams who take that seriously now will be the ones defining the market later.

8.1 Designing for Reuse and Reverse Logistics

It's easy to talk about reducing waste. It's much harder to build systems that actually bring products back once they're used. Yet in circular supply chains, reverse logistics, the ability to retrieve, repair, refurbish, or recycle products after their first life, is what makes sustainability real. Without it, even the most eco-friendly product ends up in a landfill. Without it, reuse is just a concept. And without intentional design, reverse logistics becomes an operational burden rather than a strategic advantage.

Product managers have a central role to play here. They determine how easy, or impossible, it is for a product to be reused. That power starts with form. Can the product be disassembled without damage? Are components standardized or proprietary? Is it clear what can be returned, what should be recycled, and what is meant to last? These questions shape everything from internal architecture to customer interaction.

For example, a generator casing designed to snap open with a common tool allows faster inspection and part replacement. A software system built with remote diagnostics reduces unnecessary physical returns. A modular assembly that isolates wear components enables selective upgrades rather than full-unit replacements. These aren't just efficiency wins, they're sustainability wins. Because they keep products in circulation longer, reduce the carbon cost of remanufacture, and shift the business model toward retained value rather than endless output.

But reuse doesn't succeed on design alone, it depends on return infrastructure. Many reverse logistics programs fail not because the product can't be reused, but because the organization hasn't built the system to retrieve it. Who collects the product? Where does it go? Who inspects it? What happens next? These questions require operational clarity, cross-departmental alignment, and often, collaboration with third-party logistics providers, recyclers, and remanufacturing partners.

Smart product teams work with supply chain and operations to build these pipelines in advance. They design packaging that can be reused or returned easily. They create digital triggers that notify customers when it's time for a product to be returned. They integrate QR codes or RFID tracking to simplify sorting at recovery centers. They incentivize returns through credits, loyalty points, or access to upgrades. And when the product arrives, they ensure the repair, disassembly, and refurbishment process is efficient, safe, and well-documented.

Beyond hardware, software and IoT provide massive leverage in reverse logistics. Connected products can monitor their own usage, report degradation, and trigger repair or recovery before full failure. This not only reduces downtime, it allows for predictive reverse flows. The organization can plan for reentry, balance inventory, and reintroduce parts into the supply chain with less disruption.

From a business perspective, this unlocks second-life revenue models. Instead of relying solely on first-sale margins, companies can earn value from product buy-backs, certified refurbished programs, parts resale, or long-term service subscriptions. This is already happening across industries, from heavy equipment leasing to consumer electronics to industrial pumps and modular energy storage units.

But the strategic value goes even further. In regions with rising environmental regulations or Extended Producer Responsibility (EPR) laws, the ability to reclaim products isn't just a nice-to-have, it's legally required. Companies that delay reverse logistics investment risk fines, lost contracts, and declining social license to operate. Those who build it now, however, position themselves as market leaders in sustainability, and earn the customer loyalty, compliance headroom, and operational agility that comes with it.

Designing for reuse doesn't mean every product must come back. It means designing with the option in mind. It means building pathways for products to be more than disposable. And it means embedding circular thinking not just in policy, but in blueprints, field manuals, and backend systems.

Because in a circular world, value isn't lost when the customer is done with the product, it's just waiting to be picked up again.

8.2 Tracking and Reducing Carbon Impact Through Design Choices

As climate accountability tightens globally, carbon emissions are no longer someone else's metric. Governments are regulating it. Investors are scrutinizing it. Customers are asking about it. And increasingly, carbon performance is influencing procurement decisions, brand loyalty, and market access. But where most companies struggle is not in intention, it's in translation. How do you take abstract carbon targets and bake them into product design, supply chain operations, and day-to-day development cycles?

This is where the product manager becomes a key translator. Because every material choice, every supplier relationship, every configuration tweak carries a carbon cost; often invisible, but measurable. And if those decisions go unchecked, the product quietly accumulates emissions that won't be noticed until reporting season arrives or a client demands lifecycle data.

At that point, it's too late to redesign. That's why carbon awareness must begin at the drawing board, not the dashboard.

Tracking carbon impact starts with product-level emissions modeling, a growing practice that evaluates embedded carbon across raw material extraction, manufacturing, packaging, transport, usage, and end-of-life. Tools like Life Cycle Assessment (LCA) software, Environmental Product Declarations (EPDs), and carbon-calculating plugins in design software now make this possible without slowing teams down. These tools allow product managers to model different scenarios: What happens if we switch from aluminum to recycled composite? How does ocean freight affect our footprint versus rail? What if we increase durability to reduce replacements?

This modeling empowers design-stage carbon reduction. Rather than treating emissions as a fixed outcome, product teams can actively shape it through smarter specs: lighter materials, lower-emission manufacturing processes, simplified packaging, more efficient thermal management, or energy-saving operation profiles. These small choices compound, especially when scaled across high-volume products or long-life industrial systems.

Carbon tracking also extends to supply chain configuration. Sourcing locally reduces transport emissions. Choosing suppliers powered by renewable energy reduces Scope 3 emissions. Consolidating shipments or switching to circular packaging minimizes footprint at the logistics layer. And maintaining transparent records allows these decisions to be audited, verified, and communicated credibly to stakeholders.

In more advanced organizations, these practices are paired with internal carbon pricing, a method where design and sourcing decisions are evaluated not just on cost and performance, but on their projected climate cost. This approach assigns a dollar value to every kilogram of CO_2, helping teams compare trade-offs with clearer context. For example, a cheaper part with high carbon intensity might be deprioritized in favor of a more sustainable option that delivers long-term brand, regulatory, or investment benefit.

To make this work culturally, product teams must also close the loop with carbon accountability dashboards, not just for executives, but for designers, engineers, and field teams. When carbon metrics become part of the same conversation as cost, safety, or timeline, they gain traction. Teams begin to optimize not just for unit price, but for impact-per-output. And carbon savings start showing up not as abstract victories, but as measurable contributions to the product's lifecycle performance.

Lastly, public pressure and procurement standards are accelerating this shift. Major buyers; from governments to multinationals, are now requiring carbon disclosure at the product level. Sustainability certifications increasingly include emissions thresholds. And end users are asking not just "what does it do?" but "what does it cost the planet to make it?" Product managers who can answer that question confidently, and show how it's improving, will be far more competitive in the next five years than those who cannot.

In the past, carbon performance was a reporting issue. Today, it's a design choice. And the product leaders who treat it that way will build not just cleaner supply chains, but more trusted, future-ready companies.

CHAPTER 9

Digital Transformation & Intelligent Systems in Product Lifecycle

The product lifecycle is no longer a linear path from concept to delivery, it's a dynamic, data-rich system that evolves in real time. With the rise of intelligent technologies, product management is undergoing a shift as fundamental as the assembly line once was. Digital transformation is not just changing how products are built, it's redefining how they live, learn, and respond. And for supply chain-intensive industries like energy, oil & gas, and manufacturing, this shift isn't optional. It's existential.

Digital transformation in product lifecycle management (PLM) means moving from static records and reactive tracking to continuous visibility, automated intelligence, and proactive decision-making. It's about transforming every stage, design, sourcing, production, deployment, usage, and retirement, into a system that communicates, adapts, and improves over time. And it's the product manager's role to orchestrate that shift, not just by adopting tools, but by reshaping processes around those tools.

At the foundation of this transformation is data integration. Every product generates data, usage logs, performance signals, service records, sensor inputs, environmental exposure, and supply chain timestamps. But in many organizations, that data is siloed, scattered across departments, or locked behind legacy systems. The first step in digital lifecycle intelligence is unifying this data into platforms that offer a single, searchable, real-time source of truth. Once that's achieved, product teams gain the ability to answer critical questions faster: Where is the product now? How is it performing? What's failing? What's changing? What's next?

The power of digital transformation is most visible in how it enables closed-loop systems. Instead of designing based on assumptions and adjusting based on failure, teams can design based on feedback and adjust based on behavior. Real-world performance data informs the next update. Usage patterns shape the next iteration. Maintenance frequency drives redesigns for durability or serviceability. It's no longer just about what the product is. It's about how the product evolves.

Take digital twins, for instance; virtual replicas of physical products or systems that allow teams to simulate, monitor, and test performance in real time. In energy operations, digital twins can track heat cycles on a turbine, vibration patterns in pumps, or pressure dynamics in fuel storage systems. These insights not only enable early detection of anomalies, they inform predictive maintenance, warranty planning, and safety interventions long before failure occurs. And they feed directly into the next generation of product design with surgical precision.

Another transformative force is IoT (Internet of Things), the digital nervous system of modern supply chains. With smart sensors embedded in products, field assets, and transport containers, product managers gain real-time insight into usage conditions, environmental exposure, transport delays, and user interaction. This enables smarter decisions about durability requirements, packaging design, installation protocols, and customer support. It also reduces blind spots, turning what was once reactive troubleshooting into real-time system orchestration.

But digital tools are only as valuable as the decisions they support. This is where AI and machine learning enter the picture. When layered onto connected systems, AI can detect patterns that humans miss; flagging root causes behind recurring field failures, identifying inefficiencies in distribution paths, predicting quality issues before batch completion, or optimizing restock timing based on site-specific usage rates. These aren't theoretical use cases, they are already reshaping product ecosystems across forward-thinking supply chains.

Digital transformation also redefines customer feedback loops. With intelligent systems in place, feedback is no longer limited to surveys or complaints, it includes product behavior itself. Software logs, feature usage analytics, update adoption rates, and issue escalation data all become part of the product's voice. For product managers, this turns every deployment into a learning lab. Every customer becomes a data partner. And every improvement becomes faster, more targeted, and less expensive.

Of course, all of this hinges on governance and ethics. Intelligent systems must be built with security, privacy, and transparency in mind. If a predictive feature is going to recommend a shutdown, the operator needs to know why. If a product update is based on AI-driven insights, there must be accountability for how those insights were derived. Product managers must lead not only with curiosity, but with integrity. Because the more systems learn, the more responsibility exists to ensure that learning is aligned with safety, compliance, and trust.

What makes digital transformation so powerful, and so challenging, is that it touches everything. It's not a department or software installation. It's a way of thinking. A cultural shift. A new normal where products are no longer static assets, they are active systems, evolving with input, delivering real-time value, and feeding intelligence back into the very loop that created them.

The product manager's job, in this world, is to make the loop tighter, the signals clearer, and the decisions sharper. Because in the intelligent lifecycle, iteration never stops. And the teams who design for that reality, who listen, adapt, and build with data in their hands, will not only out-innovate their competition. They'll outlast them.

Digital transformation isn't just about systems. It's about how people use those systems, how they interpret signals, respond to insights, and develop new instincts inside data-rich environments. And yet, this human shift is often overlooked. Teams are handed dashboards without context, AI-driven suggestions without explanation, and digital workflows without alignment. The result isn't transformation, it's confusion.

For product managers, digital leadership includes **building digital fluency across functions**. This means ensuring field teams know how to trust machine insights, support teams understand what data the product is generating, and compliance teams are looped in on how traceability is being digitized. Digital transformation is only as effective as the confidence of the people who interact with it. When training is shallow, resistance grows. But when teams are invited into the digital layer, shown not just the tool, but the "why", adoption takes root. Productivity rises. Risks drop. Communication improves.

Part of building that trust is changing how product documentation is managed. Traditionally, documents were static; user manuals, data sheets, and version-controlled PDFs.

But intelligent systems require living documentation. Component changes may be flagged dynamically. Performance notes may evolve based on field conditions. Compliance history may be updated based on regulation changes or new test results. This requires moving away from static repositories and into cloud-based, update-ready product documentation systems, where users always have access to the latest validated data, and where the product "tells its own story" as it evolves.

This real-time storytelling also enhances product traceability. In the past, traceability was used reactively, after a defect, during an audit, in response to a recall. But intelligent traceability turns that around. By embedding tracking from manufacturing to delivery to operation, companies can monitor not just the location of assets, but the conditions they've endured, the interventions they've received, and the patterns of usage that might affect future performance. It becomes possible to say not just *where* a product has been, but *how* it has lived. And that kind of visibility fundamentally changes warranty management, field service, compliance reporting, and design validation.

This visibility feeds into another transformational shift: the evolution of the bill of materials (BOM) from a part list to a behavioral record. Historically, the BOM was a technical artifact, what's in the product, where it was sourced, and how it's assembled. But now, that static sheet is evolving into a digital BOM that includes firmware histories, environmental exposures, component-specific service logs, and even user engagement trends. This dynamic BOM not only helps engineering teams validate assumptions, it helps business units understand cost performance across regions, use cases, and time.

For instance, a motor part that fails frequently in one region may be fine elsewhere, pointing to an environmental mismatch, not a design flaw. A software module used heavily by one customer segment may be nearly ignored by another: shaping the next feature set. These insights aren't pulled from support tickets, they're surfaced by design through intelligent lifecycle monitoring.

And that's where the real competitive advantage of digital transformation lies, not just in the automation, but in the feedback loop between people, systems, and products. Smart sensors aren't just tools, they're storytellers. Dashboards aren't just monitors, they're coaching devices. And AI isn't just a filter, it's a force multiplier for human insight.

But none of it matters without alignment. The technology must serve the product. The product must serve the user. And the team must know how to use what it learns, not just to track the past, but to shape what comes next.

Because when digital transformation is done right, the product doesn't just perform better, it teaches better. And the companies that learn from what they build will always be one iteration ahead of those that don't.

9.1 From Product Records to Product Intelligence

In traditional product environments, documentation served a defensive role. Manuals were created to satisfy regulators. Test results were stored in case of disputes. Inspection records were archived for traceability. These records were static, compliance-focused, and rarely revisited unless something went wrong. They were evidence, not intelligence.

But in digital-first environments, this mindset is evolving. Data is no longer just something to store, it's something to learn from. Every part of the product's lifecycle, from design revisions to performance data, user feedback, repair history, firmware updates, environmental exposures, and even idle time, can be captured, analyzed, and reused to strengthen the product, the process, and the business model. What emerges isn't just a set of records. It's product intelligence, a live, evolving body of knowledge that informs smarter decisions across the board.

This shift changes how product managers work. Instead of guessing what users struggle with, they see usage drop-offs. Instead of waiting for field reports, they monitor live dashboards. Instead of managing launch deadlines blindly, they prioritize based on real-time system readiness and supply chain status. Product intelligence allows for agile iteration at scale, especially critical in industrial settings where physical updates are costly and timelines are tight.

It also opens the door to predictive product management. By analyzing how similar assets perform in different environments, teams can forecast failure risks before they occur. They can preempt customer dissatisfaction before it's vocalized. They can plan updates based on degradation curves, not complaints. And perhaps most importantly, they can make product strategy decisions grounded in behavior, not assumption.

This doesn't just help product teams, it transforms how sales, support, and service organizations operate. Sales teams can pitch based on actual performance insights in comparable installations. Service teams can optimize spares based on predictive part wear. And support teams can use actual product behavior to troubleshoot, not just rely on user descriptions. The product becomes a living participant in its own success; reporting on itself, adapting to its environment, and telling teams what it needs before something goes wrong.

To enable this, organizations must invest in data architecture; not just dashboards, but the infrastructure to capture, contextualize, and route data where it can be used. This means metadata standards, API readiness, cloud integrations, and clear data ownership. It means designing products not only for function but for feedback. Sensors aren't useful if their data isn't captured. Logs aren't useful if they're unreadable. AI isn't useful if the model can't access meaningful, structured input.

But with that infrastructure in place, product intelligence becomes a competitive advantage. Companies no longer have to guess how their products are doing, they know. And they no longer have to wonder how their customers feel, they see it, reflected in behavior and system patterns in real time.

9.2 Reimagining the Bill of Materials in the Age of Intelligence

For decades, the Bill of Materials (BOM) has been treated as a simple inventory reference, a static hierarchy of components that defines what makes up a product, how it's assembled, and what needs to be ordered. It's been useful for procurement, production, and inventory tracking. But in the digital era, where products interact with their environment, update themselves, and generate data throughout their lifecycle, the BOM's role has outgrown its original function.

The modern BOM is no longer just a list, it's a behavior-aware blueprint. It doesn't only define what a product is; it reflects how that product performs, adapts, and ages in the real world. It connects materials to maintenance. Sensors to serviceability. Firmware to failure history. It captures not just structure, but **state**, and in doing so, it becomes a dynamic asset in decision-making across engineering, operations, quality, and customer support.

Reimagining the BOM begins with contextual layering. Each part isn't just identified by SKU or spec, it's tagged with performance data, supplier quality scores, lifecycle tracking, and revision history. This allows teams to see not only what's inside a product, but how that version of the part performed across multiple deployments. It enables smarter substitutions during shortages, faster root cause analysis during defects, and more confident planning during upgrades or redesigns.

It also means aligning the BOM with connected systems. Instead of being trapped inside disconnected spreadsheets or PLM systems, the modern BOM is integrated with ERP, MES, IoT, and even CRM platforms. This cross-system linkage ensures that if a part changes due to redesign, the sourcing team knows. If a component starts showing signs of systemic failure, engineering is alerted. If a firmware patch alters behavior, the BOM logs that update and its impact.

This integration turns the BOM from a cost ledger into a performance record. It's no longer just "What did we build?" but "How did it behave?", and over time, this allows for pattern recognition that guides future design. A filter that fails earlier in humid environments, a connector that loosens after repeated thermal cycling, a control board that sees firmware instability after certain updates, all of these observations become part of the BOM's living memory.

Moreover, the intelligent BOM supports **circularity**. When products are returned, remanufactured, or recycled, the BOM tells teams what materials are recoverable, what parts are eligible for reuse, and what should be retired or reprocessed. This closes the loop between design and sustainability, enabling traceability not just for compliance, but for regeneration.

And finally, the intelligent BOM enhances collaboration. Cross-functional teams can access the same source of truth, but with tailored views; engineering sees tolerances and spec revisions, procurement sees supplier links and cost histories, field teams see install instructions and service logs. No more fragmented documentation. No more version confusion. Everyone works from a shared, evolving map of what the product is and what it's becoming.

In short, the BOM is no longer a document, it's a system of intelligence. A digital reflection of the product's anatomy, history, and behavior. And the organizations that treat it this way don't just manage complexity, they master it.

Because in the age of intelligent products, success belongs to the teams that know not just what they built, but how it's living, learning, and performing long after it leaves the factory floor.

CHAPTER 10

Building High-Performance Teams for Complex Product Environments

I n high-stakes product environments, where supply chains are global, timelines are compressed, and failure isn't just costly but dangerous, tools matter. Processes matter. But nothing matters more than the team. Behind every well-executed product, there is a team of people managing friction, navigating uncertainty, and making thousands of interdependent decisions. These are not easy environments. They are dynamic, technical, politically charged, and resource-constrained. And success doesn't come from individual brilliance, it comes from collective alignment.

The myth of the lone product genius doesn't survive in complex supply chains. These ecosystems demand collaboration between product managers, engineers, operations, procurement, compliance, finance, field support, and external vendors. They require people who can span silos, translate between disciplines, and hold tension without breaking trust. Building that kind of team takes more than headcount. It takes culture, clarity, and capacity.

High-performance product teams start with role clarity. In ambiguous environments, confusion is costly. Teams need to know who owns what decision, who approves what change, who escalates what issue. When ownership is vague, bottlenecks emerge. When it's defined, momentum builds. Product managers must set clear boundaries, empowering cross-functional leaders without abdicating the core product vision.

Next comes communication fluency. In complex systems, the greatest risk is not just a bad decision, it's a misunderstood one. A change in component spec that isn't flagged to procurement. A late-stage redesign that bypasses compliance. A customer requirement that doesn't reach engineering. Each of these misalignments creates cascading damage. High-performing teams develop rituals and rhythms that prevent silence, stand-ups, design reviews, decision logs, pre-mortems, and shared planning boards that surface issues before they go critical.

But alignment isn't just about meetings, it's about shared context. In high-performance teams, everyone understands the "why" behind the roadmap. They know what the customer values, what the operation demands, what the market expects. This allows for decentralized judgment. A field engineer can make the right call during install. A sourcing specialist can flag a risk early. A QA analyst can suggest a redesign that protects against service failure. This is what makes a product team not just efficient, but resilient.

Resilience also depends on **psychological safety**. In fast-moving, failure-sensitive environments, people must feel safe to raise concerns, ask questions, and admit when something isn't working. If the team is afraid to speak up, risk hides. If feedback is ignored, improvement stalls. Product managers who want high performance must model openness. They must reward curiosity. And they must treat mistakes as data, not weakness.

Hiring also matters. High-performance teams are built intentionally, not just with technical rockstars, but with problem solvers who collaborate well under pressure. In complex product environments, humility matters more than ego. Pattern recognition beats perfectionism. Adaptability outweighs expertise locked in a single domain. Product leaders must prioritize **cross**-functional empathy and communication range in their hiring process, not just certificates or seniority.

Once in place, these teams must be nurtured. This means investing in ongoing development, not just in tools and training, but in systems thinking, leadership capacity, and business acumen. Product teams are no longer just interface owners. They're stewards of the full product lifecycle. That requires commercial awareness, supply chain fluency, and strategic thinking. The best product managers aren't just good at backlogs, they're good at seeing the entire field.

And finally, high-performance teams run on purpose. In tough environments, where constraints are constant and the workload is heavy, motivation can't come from tasks alone. It must come from meaning. Teams need to know that what they're building matters, that it will make something safer, faster, cleaner, more reliable. When people feel that purpose, they hold the line longer. They recover from setbacks faster. They push not because they have to, but because they believe in what they're shipping.

Because in the end, even the most intelligent product won't ship itself. It takes a team to carry the weight, to solve the puzzle, to smooth the friction and deliver something extraordinary in ordinary-looking packaging.

That's the real secret of complex product environments: they don't just test your processes. They test your people. And when the team is right, the product follows.

High performance isn't built once, it's maintained. In complex supply chain environments, what worked last quarter may not work next year. Processes that served a small team may break under scale. Structures built for speed may create blind spots when regulation tightens. That's why high-performing teams must be designed for adaptive capacity, not just execution. The goal is not only to deliver under pressure, but to evolve under pressure.

Adaptive teams balance structure with flexibility. They build systems that can scale, standardized checklists, templates, escalation paths, but they also know when to break the template. They don't mistake process for progress. They're disciplined enough to maintain rigor, but loose enough to shift when the situation calls for creativity. This mindset isn't accidental, it's cultivated. And it starts with how teams make decisions under stress.

In complex product environments, decision quality is the currency. You can't automate everything. You can't pre-plan every scenario. What you can do is build a culture where teams make better calls faster, with confidence and coordination. That means developing shared heuristics: "If it threatens uptime, escalate." "If a change affects compliance, pause." "If the signal is weak, simulate before rollout." These simple principles, when reinforced consistently, equip people to make aligned decisions without constant supervision.

But aligned decision-making doesn't happen in a vacuum. It requires what few teams actually cultivate: mental models of the full system. Many professionals are experts in their lane, but high-performing product teams think laterally. A designer understands procurement bottlenecks. A supply chain lead grasps software update cycles. An engineer anticipates regulatory impact. This cross-domain fluency allows teams to forecast consequence, and prevent small issues from triggering expensive, avoidable failures.

The teams that master this skill tend to invest heavily in operational storytelling. They don't just document what happened, they explain why it happened, how it was handled, and what changed. They run blameless postmortems. They analyze near-misses with the same seriousness as major failures. They normalize conversation around "what we got lucky with" as much as "what we did right." This habit doesn't just improve operations, it accelerates team maturity.

Resilience also depends on load balancing. Burnout is the silent killer of product performance. When timelines stretch endlessly and expectations mount, even elite teams erode. Product managers must learn to modulate intensity, managing momentum without running people to the edge. This means defining clear "push periods" with built-in recovery. It means setting expectations not just for output, but for sustainability. It means protecting mental bandwidth as fiercely as budget and scope.

And underneath all of this, great teams invest in internal trust. Not the soft, vague kind, but the kind built through accountability, responsiveness, and respect. In high-performance environments, trust is speed. It's what lets you challenge a peer without politics. It's what lets you flag a risk without fear. It's what lets you admit uncertainty without losing credibility. When trust runs high, feedback is faster, decisions are sharper, and delivery is smoother.

The most overlooked trait of all, though, is calm under complexity. High-performance teams don't thrive because things go well. They thrive because they don't panic when things go wrong. A vendor drops out? Adjust. A deadline slips? Recalculate. A spec fails under testing? Reframe. These teams don't spiral, they stabilize. Not by reacting harder, but by responding smarter. And that quality, steady hands in high stakes, is what ultimately separates delivery teams from leadership teams.

10.1 Hiring for Systems Thinking: Beyond Job Titles, Toward Whole-System Awareness

In complex product environments, it's not enough to hire people who are "good at their job." You need people who are good at understanding how their job fits into the whole, and how small decisions ripple across the system. This is the essence of systems thinking, a skill that, while rarely listed in job descriptions, often distinguishes merely competent teams from transformational ones.

Systems thinkers don't just execute, they anticipate consequence. They ask, "If I make this change, who else will be affected?" They think in loops, not lines. They balance speed with sustainability, autonomy with alignment, and urgency with long-term impact. These are the people who prevent process entropy, who flag risks early, who challenge assumptions not to be contrarian, but because they've seen the second and third-order effects play out before.

But hiring for this mindset takes intentionality. It's not something you discover from resumes alone. It shows up in how candidates talk about their past work. Do they focus only on what they delivered, or do they explain how their choices interacted with other teams, constraints, and systems? Do they ask questions that suggest awareness of scale, integration, and unintended consequences? Do they speak with both curiosity and accountability?

During interviews, these signals matter more than buzzwords. Strong systems thinkers will say things like:

- "We realized the redesign was efficient for our team, but it overloaded the field technicians."

- "Procurement met the price goal, but the supplier struggled with quality, so we looped in QA earlier in the process."

- "We rolled out the update, but adoption lagged, turns out the usage data looked different from the frontline reality."

These are the voices of someone who gets it. Who understands that no decision happens in isolation, and that performance isn't just a result of tasks, it's a result of interdependencies managed well.

It's also valuable to test how candidates respond to ambiguity and cross-functional scenarios. Ask them to talk through a problem with conflicting inputs, like how they'd balance cost reduction with sustainability, or prioritize a roadmap when quality, speed, and compliance are pulling in different directions. You're not looking for a perfect answer. You're looking for comfort in complexity. Can they map trade-offs? Can they pause learning before acting? Can they think upstream and downstream, not just in front of them?

And once hired, systems thinkers must be supported, not smothered. They thrive in environments that reward cross-team problem-solving, not heroics. That elevates questions, not just answers. That offers visibility into the full product ecosystem; customer insights, supply chain realities, engineering constraints, so they can connect dots that others miss.

10.2 Resilience Rituals: How Great Teams Reset, Refocus, and Regroup Without Losing Steam

Every high-performing team hits turbulence. Deadlines stretch. Stakeholders shift. A part fails under testing. A supplier disappears overnight. The measure of a strong product team isn't how well they perform when everything's going right, it's how quickly they recover when it isn't. That's where resilience rituals come in.

Resilience isn't just a personality trait or a cultural value. It's a series of practices and rhythms that allow teams to absorb setbacks without losing momentum, clarity, or confidence. These rituals don't just help teams bounce back, they help them bounce forward, learning faster, communicating more clearly, and coming out stronger with each iteration.

One of the most effective rituals is the structured pause. This could be a weekly review where the team isn't just checking status, but asking deeper questions: What friction are we tolerating that we shouldn't? Where are we reacting instead of responding? What is draining energy or slowing clarity? These aren't venting sessions, they're operational resets. The goal is not to find blame, but to regain perspective.

Another ritual is the no-judgment postmortem. After a launch, a missed milestone, or a near-failure, resilient teams come together to dissect, not defend. What did we assume that turned out wrong? What did we get right by accident? What signals did we ignore? In high-pressure environments, it's tempting to bury what went wrong. But resilient teams document and discuss those cracks early, because they know silence doesn't protect performance. It just protects fragility.

There are also human-centered resets, moments that prioritize the emotional bandwidth of the team. This might mean slowing the sprint pace after a major push. Rotating ownership of recurring stressors like vendor calls or stakeholder comms. Blocking time for deep work so people can recalibrate. High-functioning teams know that burnout is a systems failure, not a character flaw, and they design rhythms that honor both urgency and rest.

Even language can be ritualized. Great teams normalize phrases like:

- "Let's circle back before this calcifies."
- "What are we solving *for* here?"
- "Are we still designing for the constraint that matters most?"
- "Does this need to be perfect, or just safe enough to test?"

These aren't just clever one-liners, they're cultural anchors. They remind teams to step out of panic mode and back into systems thinking.

Another powerful resilience tool is the "fail safely" simulation. Some product teams run tabletop scenarios where they role-play what happens if something fails, what's the backup? What's the recovery time? Who needs to know first? This kind of rehearsal lowers response time when real issues arise, reduces blame spirals, and boosts collective confidence. Everyone knows the drill, and nobody is frozen when pressure hits.

About the Author

Olisaemeka Adigwe is a multidisciplinary product and operations strategist with over a decade of experience driving innovation, efficiency, and resilience in the supply chain and energy sectors. With a background in engineering and a career that spans manufacturing, oil & gas, and digital transformation, he brings a systems-level perspective to product management, one that fuses technical depth with operational pragmatism.

He is a COREN-certified engineer, a certified project management professional (PMP), and a recognized supply chain management specialist. His career has been defined by a unique ability to navigate complex environments, translating field-level realities into strategic product decisions that reduce downtime, improve quality, and enable sustainable growth.

From developing predictive maintenance frameworks for high-risk energy assets to leading cross-functional product teams through large-scale digital transformations, he has consistently delivered impact where it matters most, on the ground, in the field, and across the supply chain.

He is passionate about building intelligent systems that evolve with data, supporting teams that thrive under complexity, and embedding sustainability and safety into every phase of the product lifecycle.

This book is an extension of that mission, a practical, experience-driven guide for the next generation of product leaders working in high-stakes, supply chain-intensive industries.

He lives in Nigeria and consults globally. He continues to mentor early-career professionals and contribute to industry conversations on product innovation, operational excellence, and responsible technology.

References

1. Abernathy, F. H., Dunlop, J. T., Hammond, J. H., & Weil, D. (2000). *A stitch in time: Lean retailing and the transformation of manufacturing, Lessons from the apparel and textile industries*. Oxford University Press.

2. Axelrod, R., & Cohen, M. D. (2000). *Harnessing complexity: Organizational implications of a scientific frontier*. Free Press.

3. Brown, T. (2009). *Change by design: How design thinking creates new alternatives for business and society*. Harvard Business Press.

4. Christopher, M. (2016). *Logistics & supply chain management* (5th ed.). Pearson Education.

5. Deloitte Insights. (2023). *The future of the product: Accelerating transformation through product lifecycle intelligence*. Retrieved from https://www2.deloitte.com

6. Gershenfeld, N., Gershenfeld, A., & Cutcher-Gershenfeld, J. (2017). *Designing reality: How to survive and thrive in the third digital revolution*. Basic Books.

7. Harvard Business Review. (2021). *The new product mindset: Shifting from output to outcome*. Harvard Business Publishing.

8. Kiron, D., & Schatsky, D. (2020). *Using AI to accelerate product development*. MIT Sloan Management Review. Retrieved from https://sloanreview.mit.edu

9. Liker, J. K. (2004). *The Toyota Way: 14 management principles from the world's greatest manufacturer*. McGraw-Hill.

10. McKinsey & Company. (2022). *Digital twins: Creating a bridge between the physical and digital*. Retrieved from https://www.mckinsey.com

11. O'Reilly, C. A., & Tushman, M. L. (2016). *Lead and disrupt: How to solve the innovator's dilemma*. Stanford Business Books.

12. Porter, M. E., & Heppelmann, J. E. (2014). *How smart, connected products are transforming competition*. Harvard Business Review, 92(11), 64–88.

13. Raworth, K. (2017). *Doughnut economics: Seven ways to think like a 21st-century economist*. Chelsea Green Publishing.

14. Schmidt, J., & Wagner, S. M. (2019). Blockchain and supply chain: *Conceptual framework and empirical evidence*. International Journal of Production Research, 57(7), 2117–2135.

15. Sterman, J. D. (2000). *Business dynamics: Systems thinking and modeling for a complex world*. Irwin/McGraw-Hill.

16. Womack, J. P., & Jones, D. T. (2003). *Lean thinking: Banish waste and create wealth in your corporation* (2nd ed.). Free Press.

www.ingramcontent.com/pod-product-compliance
Lightning Source LLC
LaVergne TN
LVHW091534070526
838199LV00001B/59